BLACK HEROES of the MARTIAL ARTS

COVER: TAIMAK

Published by
A&B PUBLISHERS GROUP
1000 Atlantic Avenue, Brooklyn, New York 11238

Library of Congress Cataloging-in-Publication Data

Van Clief, Ron.
    The black heroes of the martial arts/by Ron Van Clief
        p.   cm.
    Includes index.
    ISBN 1-881316-87-4. — ISBN 1-881316-78-5   (pbk.)
    1.   Afro-American martial artists —Biography. I. Title.
GV1113.A2V36   1996
796.8' 092' 2   94-46817
[B] —DC20   CIP

First Edition

Printed in the United States of America

RON VAN CLIEF, Ph.D.

FIVE TIME WORLD CHAMPION

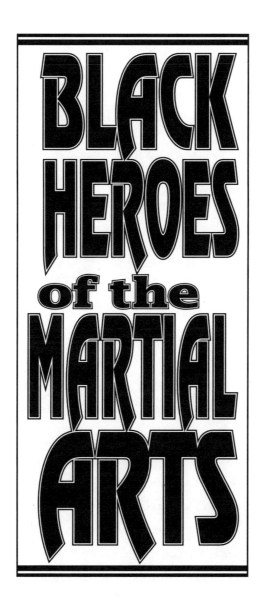

A&B PUBLISHERS GROUP, BROOKLYN, NEW YORK

Dedication

To all my children, Lissette, Ronald

and

Esteban

I love you very much!

SPECIAL THANKS

DESIGN: *Dorria Ameen*

COVER PHOTOGRAPH & CONCEPT: *Ron Larson*

EDITING & POST PRODUCTION: *Maxwell Taylor*

BLACK DRAGON MOVIE STILLS COURTESY

OF THE RON VAN CLIEF ARCHIVES

ACTION ARTS MAGAZINE PICTURE CREDITS

Sifu Alan Goldberg AND *Al Sussman*

Serafim Karalexis AND *Yeo Ban Yee*

A&B PUBLISHERS GROUP

Taimak, KYOSHI 7TH DEGREE RED BELT

Ron Van Clief Jr., SHIHAN 6TH DEGREE RED BELT

FACING PAGE & OVERLEAF:
RON VAN CLIEF,
THE BLACK DRAGON

CONTENTS

CHAPTER ONE

AN INTRODUCTION TO THE
BLACK MARTIAL ARTS EXPERIENCE

Who are the black heroes of the martial arts? These are rare individuals that have succeeded in a racist and hostile environment to become real role models for their people. From the beginning of time, the black man has always been a great warrior. From ancient Egyptian civilizations, black people have been scientists, scholars, leaders, warriors and builders. Today, Jesse Owens, FloJo Jackie Joiner, Muhammad Ali, Joe Louis, Sugar Ray Leonard, Mike Tyson, and many others, light the way for our people as great athletic role models. In my thirty-nine years of martial arts study, I have never seen any martial artist that has compared to the black man, a born athlete at the top level of professional sports. We were kings in Africa. Then, we became slaves in America. Drugs and crime have taken over our neighborhoods. Violence has become an epidemic problem in black culture. I dedicate this book to the men and women that have inspired me to persevere in the martial arts.

My first teacher, Grandmaster Moses Powell, taught me the art of jiu-jitsu. Jiu-jitsu means the capabilities of the soft. I grew up in Brooklyn, New York, in the 1940's. As a youth in the 1950's, I was first introduced to the martial arts at the St. Johns Community Center. There, I met Grandmasters Moses Powell and Ronald Duncan. They were my role models. Until then, I only had non black role models to emulate. They gave me pride in myself and being black. From them, I learned how awesome the black man is. Grandmaster Ronald Duncan, the father of American Ninjitsu, was incredible to watch. He taught me the basics of ninjitsu. Ninjitsu is the art of stealth. Weaponry played a large part in ninjitsu. It was like watching Superman and Batman

FACING PAGE:

MOSES POWELL, JONATHAN STEWART AND RON VAN CLIEF

11

TAIMAK, IRON MIKE TYSON
AND RON VAN CLIEF

Photograph by
Sensei Kwame Adansi Bona

at the same time. In the late 1950's, I was first exposed to the Chinese kung fu movies by my cousin, Kirk Wood. We would go to Chinatown and watch two or three movies in a row. I was addicted to kungfu movies. As a teenager, I knew that I wanted to someday be a master of the martial arts. In 1960, I joined the United States Marine Corps. This was the start of a whole new life for me, the life of a black martial artist.

My first overseas tour of duty was on Okinawa. Okinawa is where karate originated. Karate is the art of the empty hand combat. On Okinawa, I studied Okinawa-te and Kenpo. These arts came from Chinese and African roots. I made black belt on Okinawa. Later I was transferred to the Philippines. In the Philippines, I learned Arnis and Kali. These arts revolve around the blade and stick. Later on, I was stationed in Vietnam. It was in Vietnam that I began to understand the life of the warrior. My only brother, Larry, was killed in combat. My mother, Doris, said to me there is no way a black man should go into the military. I served my country from 1960 to 1965. When I returned home, I was just another nigger. In Vietnam, racist white boys killed my black brothers in combat. There is no reason to fight the enemy and be shot in the back by racists.

My first experience in the Marine Corps was a Drill Instructor calling me a nigger. He then punched me in the face. The 1960's was a bad time to be a black person. Boot

TAIMAK *(The Last Dragon)*

Camp was horrendous for everyone, especially the black man. Racism was the order of the day. Most restaurants would not serve a black man. In 1963, I was hung by my neck and hospitalized by a group of white racists in Kingston, North Carolina. I spent four months at the Naval Hospital on the base. For surviving this vicious attack, I was transferred to Southeast Asia. In 1965, I received an Honorable Discharge from the United States Marine Corps. Racism is a plague that should be eliminated.

After five and a half years in the Marine Corps, I entered the New York Transit Police Academy. It was during this year that I had the honor of meeting Tom LaPuppet, the

first black man inducted into the Hall of Fame. That year, he won the All American Championship at Madison Square Garden. He was truly awesome. Tom and I became good friends and martial arts brothers. Grandmaster George Cofield was Tom's teacher of the style of Shotokan. Tong Dojo was the headquarters of the finest karate fighters on the east coast. Grandmaster Cofield was a great teacher and role model in the black community. I will never forget the lessons he taught me. This period started my years of competition that lasted until 1993. It was in 1966 that my only brother, Larry, died in combat in Vietnam. He was a decorated U. S. Army infantryman. My life would never be the same again. Martial arts became my only life. Training became my religion.

In 1969, I won my first World Championship at the New York Coliseum. The Japan Exposition World Championship was a two day competition. I fought eleven times and emerged the Grand Champion. This is the proudest moment of my martial arts career. My dream had come true, winning first place in the middleweight division and the overall Grand Championship. The years of dedication had finally paid off. Shortly after I quit the Police Department, I opened my first commercial karate school. This started the most intense period of training of my life. From 1965 to 1992, I competed in the All American Championships 25 times, winning first place in my weight division eight different times.

RON VAN CLIEF AT THE WORLD CHAMPIONSHIPS IN HONG KONG

In 1981, I wrote my first book, *The Manual of the Martial Arts*. What good was my knowledge if I didn't give it to someone else? My teacher, Grandmaster Peter Urban told me a qualified master must be published. I received my Red Belt Masters Degree in 1971. During the 1970's, I traveled to Hong Kong, Thailand, Korea and the Philippines to star in five feature films as "The Black Dragon." The Hong Kong Chinese Martial Arts Association promoted me to the level of Grandmaster in 1975. In 1981, I was inducted into the All American Hall of Fame. I traveled to Hong Kong and tried my hand at full contact fighting in 1982. I had only fought in point tournaments until this time. Full contact is a total different story. I placed second place

14

at the Hong Kong World Free Fighting Championship. This was the first and only time in my whole martial arts career that I was knocked out. In Hong Kong, there are no rules except attacking the eyes and throat. I was kicked in the head while on the floor. In America, you cannot kick an opponent while he is on the canvas. This type of contact is perfectly acceptable in the Orient. My injuries required ear surgery. I lost my hearing in my left ear for several months. Thank God, my injuries were not permanent. It was a very enlightening experience that I will remember always.

I returned to the United States in 1983. The Professional Karate Organization inducted me into the Karate Hall of Fame in 1983. I officially retired from competition and started teaching full time. My concentration was on producing high quality students. At that time, I was operating 18 school for Self Defense Industries. In 1985, I was hired by Mr. Berry Gordy of Motown to choreograph *The Last Dragon*. The director, Mr. Michael Schultz, was one of my teachers at the Negro Ensemble Company. They were looking for

RON VAN CLIEF AND
MR. BERRY GORDY

a young, black man to star in their martial arts fantasy feature. The rest is history. My student, Taimak, won the role of Bruce Leroy. This film was the first mainstream film that portrayed a black man as a hero. A wonderful screenplay, written by Louis Venosta, catapulted Taimak into international stardom. Previous to this, only Jim Kelly and myself were the black martial arts heroes of the big screen. Before this, black men were only cast as villains. Thanks again, Mr. Gordy for your contributions to the black martial arts experience.

In 1988 and 1989, I won the All American Karate Championships at Madison Square Garden in New York City. Freefighting at forty-five years old is quite different than when you are twenty years old. The only real difference is that you have an old machine with an upgraded microprocessor. It is harder to get and keep in shape. Maintenance is the most important part of the martial arts cycle. Aerobics and Progressive Resistance are important to the physical maintenance of the body. Weights are really good therapy to isolated muscle groups.

CHAPTER TWO
THE GRAND MASTERS

T he Grand Masters are the source of accumulated knowledge for the Afro-American martial artist. Just like the chief and wise men of the African tribes, the knowledge is passed on to the next generation. Today, the Grand Masters give us the oral history of the black man in the martial arts. Grandmaster Moses Powell was the first real master of the martial arts that I had ever seen. A Grand Master understands the principle and theory of martial arts applications. Martial arts is not just a physical form of self defense, it is an internalization process that promotes self development. The basic tenets of martial arts dictate that you become better everyday in every way. Chaka Zulu told me that a martial artist should be gentle in life and ferocious in combat. A Grand Master has studied their particular art for a minimum of twenty years. He or she is a teacher, parent, builder and warrior. A Grand Master possesses special powers that border on the superhuman. Superhuman can be translated to mean supernormal. Supernormal is the ability to do things that seem incredible. In the martial arts we are taught that nothing is impossible! These are the Grand Masters of the Martial Arts.

FACING PAGE:

RON VAN CLIEF AND
DRAGON LEE

ABOVE:

R. GUY, M. POWELL,
J. DAVIS, R. JETER, B. DAVIS
AND A. MUHAMMAD

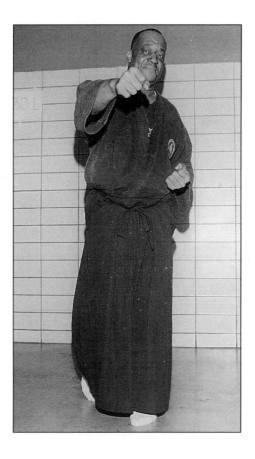

GRANDMASTER MOSES POWELL

Grandmaster Moses Powell, a 10th Degree Red Belt, started his training in the martial arts over 40 years ago. He is the first black man to teach the F.B.I. and Secret Service. His dojo, on Atlantic Ave. in Brooklyn, New York, was were thousands of black youths started their martial education. His teacher, Grandmaster Florendo Visitacion, is amazing at the young age of 83. Sanuces, his unique form of jiu-jitsu, combines many different forms of martial arts including Karate, Arnis, and Weaponry. His main emphasis is on realistic self defense tactics. Grandmaster Powell was my first teacher. He showed me the way of the martial arts. Shihan Little John Davis brought me to the St. Johns Community Center to watch class. Watching Moses Powell flying through the air and rolling out on one finger was incredible. He was capable of doing a handstand on one finger. Watching him was like seeing a fine tuned machine functioning. Shihan Little John Davis is a multi-world champion in fighting and form. Grandmaster Powell has taught thousands of students in America and overseas. He is truly a Grandmaster of the highest order, a member of the Black Belt Hall of Fame and World Karate Hall of Fame. I am very proud to have studied with Grandmaster Powell. He is an absolute testament of the black man's prowess in the martial arts.

FACING PAGE / ABOVE:

MOSES POWELL

19

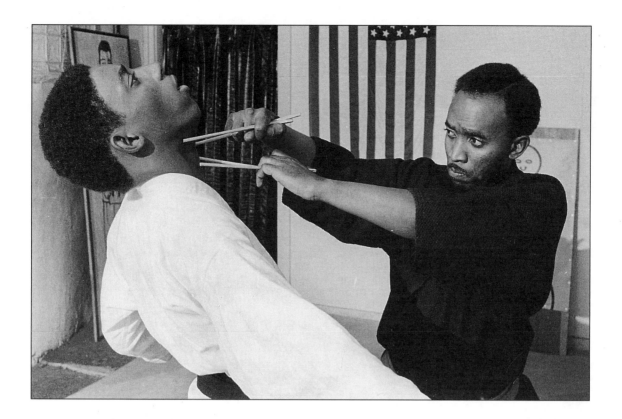

GRANDMASTER RONALD DUNCAN

FACING PAGE / ABOVE:

RON DUNCAN

Grandmaster Ronald Duncan is the father of American Ninjitsu. He is an ex-marine who studied the arts of jiu-jitsu and Ninjitsu in Okinawa and Japan. For over 40 years, he has lead the field of ninjitsu in America. He is a member of the Black Belt Hall of Fame and the World Martial Arts Hall of Fame. I met Grandmaster Duncan in the late 1950's, just before I joined the United States Marine Corps. His mastery of traditional and contemporary weaponry is legendary. He has produced thousands of students in America and overseas. The St. Johns Community Center, in Brooklyn, was were I first saw Grandmaster Duncan. I was amazed by his martial arts technology and spirituality. He is indeed a living legend in the martial arts world. Professor Duncan earned a Black Belt in Hakko Ryu Jiujitsu, Dai-nippon Jiu-jitsu, Nippon sosusitti Ryu, Kin Dai Gao, Kodokan Judo, Aikido, Aiki-jitsu, Kempo, Chi-chi-su, Kobujitsu and Shinobino-jitsu (popularly known as Ninjitsu). His teachers were all legendary men; Charlie Neal, Earnie Cates, Tatsuo Uzaki and Don Draeger. Professor Duncan has taught Special Troops, Navy S.E.A.L. Teams, Law Enforcement Agencies and various government agencies in foreign countries. He is also an accredited expert in firearms competition shooting, with pistols, shotguns and automatic weapons. Though Ninjitsu is still more or less shrouded in mystery, Professor Duncan's lectures, demonstrations and classes bring it into the light of contemporary understanding.

GRANDMASTER GEORGE COFIELD

FACING PAGE / ABOVE:

GEORGE COFIELD

Grandmaster George Cofield, 9th degree Black Belt, is the founder of the infamous Tong Dojo. He has taught greats like Tom LaPuppet and Hawk Frazier. In the 1960's and 1970's, the members of the Tong Dojo were unbeatable. I had the honor of studying with Grandmaster Cofield and achieved the level of 5th degree black belt in the Shotokan style of karate. George was the first instructor to use codes like step ladder for jump kicks. For over 40 years, Grandmaster Cofield was a pillar of the black martial arts world. A student of Sensei Maynard Minor, he was trained in the traditional form of Shotokan. He was an innovator that changed the traditional style to adapt to the black man. His colors were the red, green and black of the African liberation flag. Many of his students went on to become local and national champions. The Tong Dojo in Brooklyn, New York, will always be a trademark of the black martial arts experience. Grandmaster Cofield is responsible for teaching his unique form of Shotokan to thousands of students all over the world. He is a member of the Black Belt Hall of Fame and the World Karate Hall of Fame.

GRANDMASTER OWEN WATSON

Grandmaster Owen Sakata Watson is the founder of the Twin Dragon Martial Arts System. He has studied the martial arts for over 25 years. Owen is a 10 time United States Champion in karate. In the 1960's, Owen and I were students of Grandmaster Frank Ruiz of the Nisei Goju System. He was known for his fierce fighting style that included various elements of kung fu and karate jitsu. We fought each other over a hundred times. In the 1960's and 1970's, Owen was one of the best fighters in the United States. Obosan had the fierceness of a tiger combined with the cunning of a wolf. He was quite remarkable as a fighter in the ring and on the street. We traveled all over the United States and Canada fighting in tournaments. Presently, he lives and teaches his art, Sum Lung Miu, in Reno, Nevada.

GRANDMASTER JONATHAN STEWART

Grandmaster Stewart began his studies of martial arts when he was 7 years old, in the arts of boxing and judo. He completed an advance Instructor Training Course in 1960, and became an instructor in a program sponsored by the United States Department of Defense and the Department of State. In 1966, he went to the Republic of China and studied the Chinese Art of boxing (Wu-Tzu), Tai Chi Chuan, and martial medicine through the art of acupressure and acupuncture, under the supervision of Grandmaster Laio Chien. He received a Masters Certificate from the government of the Republic of Taiwan for his performances and participation with Chinese and Taiwanese school children, and military and civilian personnel in the martial arts. Professor Stewart has taught at Brooklyn College and Manhattan College. In 1988, he received the Alt Heidelberg-Schlok und Alts Brucke Certificate. He has traveled extensively throughout America, Africa and Europe teaching the martial arts to private citizens, police and military personnel. In 1990, he established chapters of the Stewart American Martial Arts System in Poland, Russia, Belgium and Austria. In 1991, he received the World Martial Arts Hall of Fame Humanitarian Lifetime Achievement Award and was inducted into the World Martial Arts Black Belt Hall of Fame. In January 1992, he received the rank of 10th Dan in Vee-Jitsu from Supreme Grandmaster Florendo Visitacion. Professor Stewart's demonstrations are crowd pleasers. His technique is clear, smooth and effective. Whenever you see him perform it will be an enriching experience.

FACING PAGE:

JONATHAN STEWART

GRANDMASTER CHAKA ZULU

In 1949, at the age of 10, Grandmaster Zulu joined the Harlem Boy's Club where he was introduced to the American martial sport of boxing. This would be the start of a long martial arts career. At the age of 11, Zulu was introduced to James Elliot, who was a second degree black belt in the art of Judo. Zulu studied under Sensei Elliot and eventually achieved the rank of brown belt. Around this time, Zulu decided to join the United States Marine Corps. This became the core foundation of his development as a man and martial artist. In the Marine Corps, Zulu was taught by several individuals in the arts of war. He was also asked by his superiors to teach Judo. He set out to be the best warrior that he could imagine himself. He became fluent in the use of the flame thrower, the bow, and a qualified expert with firearms. Upon leaving the Marine Corps, Zulu continued to study the martial arts on his own. As the head of security at the night club, the Electric Circus, Master Zulu hired an all black belt staff. I met Zulu in 1965, when he hired me as security at the Electric Circus. Zulu and I became friends and roommates. Zulu has and always will be an inspiration to me. We were dojo brothers in the same dojo for seven years. Grandmaster Frank Ruiz was the founder of the Nisei Goju System and a former marine. Nisei prided itself on domination in sport karate from the 1960's to the 1970's. Master Zulu excelled at fighting and won many championships, never taking less than second place, usually taking first. Zulu is one of the most incredible kata performers I have ever seen. Later, Zulu was invited to take instruction under Grandmaster Moses Powell. Master Zulu achieved the rank of 3rd degree black belt, the highest rank Grandmaster Powell had ever given to anyone outside his own system. Master Zulu integrated his training, incorporating his own innovations to improve his art. His main concern was self defense and this is reflected in all of his teachings. In the early 1980's, Master Zulu realized that he was no longer teaching solely one art. Instead, he was teaching something unique. He found that it was necessary to change the name of his teachings. In 1984, he came up with the name Zujitsu: The art of Zulu. Zujitsu has since spread. Late in 1992, the Zujitsu Martial Arts Federation was formed. In 1993, Grandmaster Zulu was inducted into the Karate Hall of Fame and promoted to the level of 10th degree Red Belt. The Zujitsu system as spread to twelve affiliated schools in five different countries. What we study today has been passed down through Grandmaster Zulu to us.

FACING PAGE / ABOVE:

CHAKA ZULU

GRANDMASTER RON AUSTIN

Grandmaster Ronald Austin is the founder of the Jaribu System of martial arts. This African-American system has been taught by Kyoshi Austin for over 27 years. He has produced many local and national champions. An honorable Grandmaster with amazing referee skills, he sees everything. I have fought many of his students. He is a truly honest man. In 1991, I won the United States Championship. He was the Chief Referee of my final match against one of his black belt students. In my over 40 years of experience, I have never met a more honorable referee than Ron Austin. He would always be harder on his students than any referee would ever be. My respect for his talents and skills is absolute. Many times, my students faced him at tournaments. I knew they would always be treated fairly. Cheating was a constant element in the tournaments of the 1960's. Many of the best fighters would not even enter tournaments because of the constant cheating. Remember, no matter what, the fighters know who won the fight. There are basically five areas of tournament competition: Fighting, Kata, Weapons, Self Defense and Breaking. Kyoshi Austin has been working on a national scoring system for the martial arts for three decades. There should be an amateur and professional league that would govern tournament procedures, a non-political organization that would represent the martial arts. I will always hold Kyoshi Austin in high esteem. Kyoshi Austin is a great teacher capable of imparting not only the physical skills, but the true essence of martial arts.

FACING PAGE:

RON AUSTIN

GRANDMASTER SKIPPER INGHAM

Grandmaster Skipper Ingham started his martial arts training in 1944. In over forty years of martial arts study, he has reached the level of 10th Degree Red Belt. Kendo, Nisei Goju Karate, Japanese Goju Karate, Judo, Iaido and Jiu jitsu are some of the arts in which he has attained the level of black belt. Grandmaster Ingham lives in Bermuda and promotes the Bermuda International Championships once a year. It is the biggest tournament in the Caribbean. Skipper and I studied the art of Nisei Goju under Grandmaster Frank Ruiz in the 1960's. In 1993, Skipper won the All Goju Championships in New York City. He is an excellent martial artist and teacher. Grandmaster Ingham has traveled from Russia to Australia with the TransWorld Oil Team. As coach of the team, Skipper keeps in excellent shape. He is a member of the Martial Arts Hall of Fame.

FACING PAGE / ABOVE:

SKIPPER INGHAM

GRANDMASTER THOMAS LAPUPPET

FACING PAGE / ABOVE:

TOM LAPUPPET

Grandmaster LaPuppet is the first black man inducted into the Black Belt Hall of Fame. He is a master of Shotokan Karate and Jiujitsu. I met Tom in the 1960's, at the All American Championships in New York. He taught me the essence of Shotokan kata. Tom is responsible for karate in the Olympics. Grandmaster LaPuppet has been a driving force in Amateur Athletics. Tom was an amazing fighter in the karate ring. His self defense and kata are precise and explosive. He is a credit to the black man in the martial arts. He is certainly a legend in his own time. Tom and I were roommates in the East Village. We worked together as bouncers at the Electric Circus and The Dom. These were famous night spots in the 1960's, the era of the disco. After retiring from the New York Fire Department, Tom continued developing many local and national organizations governing amateur karate. In the 1970's, Tom starred in several martial arts films such as *The Super Weapon* and *Force Four*. Grandmaster LaPuppet has recently been inducted to the World Hall of Fame for his lifetime of contributions to the martial arts. I will never forget the lessons learned from Grandmaster LaPuppet. Semper Fi, my Aquarian brother.

GRANDMASTER RON JETER

FACING PAGE / ABOVE:

RON JETER

Grandmaster Ron Jeter is known internationally as The Master Blaster. For over three decades, his ice, cinderblock, brick and glass breaks have amazed audiences. The Master Blaster breaks cinderblocks as if they were pebbles. He attacks the bricks as if they were alive. His spirit is evident in the awesome power revealed. For over twenty five years, he has been a student of the martial arts. Ron's style encompasses Goju Karate, Judo, Jiujitsu and Kobujitsu (weaponry). I met Ron in the late 1960's, at Preston Carter's Tournament in Trenton, New Jersey. He broke five cinderblocks and three giant blocks of ice. The stage shook when he blasted the cinderblocks with his fist. It was truly an exciting experience for me. That is how I met the Master Blaster. Later, Ron created a network of schools in the tri-state area. He is a member of the World Martial Arts Hall of fame.

38

CHAPTER THREE
THE YOUNG MASTERS

T he Young Masters are the teachers of the martial arts. They teach by example. Modern day masters teach and compete in tournaments and exhibitions. A master has studied over ten years as a minimum. Master level starts at 3rd degree black belt and continues to the 6th degree black belt. There are hundreds of different styles of martial arts today. In days of old, the masters never competed. In true martial arts, we continue to learn from white belt to red belt. The process of learning never stops. If the Grand Masters are the chiefs then the Masters are the tribal council members. In the martial arts, the more you learn, the less you really know. You can never learn everything. The Masters are to be respected. The Grand Masters are to be venerated. These are the teachers of the manhood rites today.

FACING PAGE :

WESLEY SNIPES

ABOVE :

TAIMAK KICKING PAD

MASTER DOUG PIERRE

Guro Doug Pierre is a disciple of Grandmaster Remy Presas. Grandmaster Presas is the founder of Modern Arnis. Modern Arnis is the Filipino art of stick, blade and empty hand combat. Master Pierre is a two time World Arnis champion. He has promoted the first full contact stick fighting tournament in New York. I studied Modern Arnis with Grandmaster Presas in the Philippines during the 1970's. Master Pierre has studied the martial arts for over twenty years, having attained black belt levels in karate and kung fu. Master Pierre lives and teaches his art in New York City at the Budo Kai Kan.

MASTER RICO GUY

Master Rico Guy is a complete martial artist. He has received black belt degrees in Kempo, Jiu-Jitsu, Judo, Kendo, Iaido and Karate. He is the first black man to receive a black belt in Kendo and is the highest ranked black man in Iaido in the United States. Master Guy has been teaching for over twenty-five years and has been a continuing student of the arts for over 35 years. He studied under Masters Yoshiteru Otani, Frank Ruiz, Chris De Basi, M. Nagashi and Billy Davis. He is the founder of U. S. Budo Kai Kan school in existence in Manhattan for the past twenty years. Presently, there are twelve schools affiliated with the organization in the United States and overseas.

LEFT:

RICO WITH SWORD

ABOVE:

RICO WITH SON

MASTER JOHN DAVIS

Shihan John Davis studied with Grandmaster Moses Powell for over thirty years. He is responsible for my meeting Grandmaster Powell in the late 1950's, at St. Johns Community Center. John opened to door to the martial arts for me. I will always be grateful to him for enhancing my life. He is a truly awesome competitor and demonstrator. Watching John demonstrate self defense is an enriching experience. John is really the "super weapon," a former world champion in fighting and forms. In the 1960's, he was truly awesome to watch. When you would see him compete, you would feel sorry for his opponent. He would send chills up your spine. He is a member of the World Karate Hall of Fame and the World Professional Karate Organization Hall of Fame. He will always be my martial arts brother. Thanks for everything, John.

MASTER DANNY GWIRA "THE AFRICAN DRAGON"

Master Danny Gwira started his training in the martial arts over 20 years ago. He started his study in Ghana, West Africa, in the form of Judo and Tae Kwon Do. In 1973, he came to America and started studying with Kyoshi Ron Van Clief. In 1979, he established the first Chinese Goju school in Accra. The school had over 900 students. Danny has traveled internationally, spreading the Chinese Goju doctrine. In 1980, he established African Goju, an eclectic style based on the Chinese Goju System. Master Gwira has spread the style of African Goju to Nigeria, Liberia, Ivory Coast, Togo and Senegal.

LEFT / ABOVE:

DANNY GWIRA

MASTER ANTHONY RICHARD MUHAMMAD

Master Anthony Richard Muhammad has been a student of Grandmaster Moses Powell for over 20 years. His style of Sanuces Ryu is a combination of Jiu-jitsu, V-jitsu and Karate do. Shihan Muhammad is a Correction Officer in New York City. The When Worlds Collide Dojo is the headquarters of the Sanuces and Kumite-ryu Systems. Master Muhammad is a six degree Black Belt in Sanuces Ryu. He is a credit to his race and the world martial arts community.

Master Darryl Sarjeant

Master Darryl Sarjeant is the founder of Kamau-ryu, an Afro-American system of self defense. A student of the martial arts for over two decades, Darryl teaches his style at his dojo in Staten Island, New York. This karate-jitsu form encompasses a variety of martial arts styles including Jiu-jitsu, Zujitsu, Goju karate, Shotokan karate and V-jitsu. He is in constant demand to teach seminars and workshops nationally. He is a fifth degree black belt in Chinese Goju Karate and Aikijitsu.

ABOVE:

DARRYL SARJEANT

MASTER MALACHI LEE

Master Malachi Lee was a giant of a man, not only in stature but an extraordinary karate man. We fought many times in the 1960's and 1970's. At 6' 9", he was indeed an awesome opponent. Malachi studied and taught the art of Isshinryu Karate. This unique form of karate was originated on the island of Okinawa. It is a traditional style that placed emphasis on weaponry. Because of his height and reach, he was hard to get to. At the East Coast Championship, we fought two sudden death overtimes. Finally, he kicked me in the chest with a front kick. The kick propelled me off the stage into the audience. He beat me by one point. Malachi's untimely death saddened the martial arts world. He will be greatly missed by his students and the martial arts world. They called our match the David and Goliath match. Looking up at him, towering over me, was really something to see. Malachi was posthumously inducted to the World Karate Hall of Fame.

MASTER SEKWII SHA

Master Sha is a graduate of the American College of Dans and a certified massage, physical therapist. He is a graduate of National Institute and the College of Physical Therapy and Swedish Massage based in Chicago. Master Sha has over 26 years of practice and experience worldwide in massage and physical therapy. He has been training and teaching people from all walks of life in Scientific Metaphysical Technology, as well as, Martial Artistry and Physical Fitness. Master Sha is the founder of the Shanando Style, and a former New York State champion in sparring, forms and weapons. He is a disciple of Grandmaster Peter G. Urban, 10th Degree Red Belt, for over 20 years.

MASTER LINDA RAMZY RANSON

Sensei Ranson is a Black Belt in Jiu-jitsu. She started her martial arts training at the age of 38. A consultant to the New York City Task Force Against Sexual Assault, she lectures and presents workshops on self defense all over the country. She has appeared on *20/20* and *Geraldo*. The Women's Empowerment Self Defense Academy is run by Linda in New York. She teaches at Yale, Princeton and Dartmouth University. Sensei Ranson travels internationally, demonstrating her unique form of karate-jitsu. Her common sense, self defense is simple and effective. Since 1986, she has been teaching her art. Linda is the Self Defense and Rape Prevention Chairperson for the National Women's Martial Arts Federation and has given self defense seminars extensively in the United States and Europe. She is a licensed paramedic, emergency medical technician and CPR instructor. Sensei Ranson is fifty years young and a credit to the martial arts community.

48

MASTER ROBERT CROSSON

Master "Sugar" Crosson has studied the art of Sanuces Jiu-jitsu under the legendary Little John Davis. He was the star of the first documentary on martial arts from the black perspective, *The Super Weapon*. A world class champion and international performer, he is in constant demand for demonstrations and seminars. Sugar has amazing gymnastic abilities and is a total showman. With over twenty years of training behind him, he is something to see. In *The Super Weapon*, he displays his unique form of jiu-jitsu. Sugar-ryu is his own eclectic form of martial arts that he has made internationally famous. A member of the New York Board of Education School Safety Officers Department, he is constantly involved with youth and demonstrates a positive role model. The World Professional Karate Organization inducted him into the Hall of Fame in 1985.

LEFT / ABOVE:

ROBERT CROSSON

MASTER RALPH MITCHELL

ABOVE / RIGHT:

RALPH MITCHELL

Master Ralph Mitchell is member of the Eastern United Kung fu Federation and the World Eskrima Kali Arnis Federation. He is a certified instructor of Doce Pares System of Filipino Arts, Progressive Fighting Systems and Southern Chinese Boxing, and a student of Grandmaster Gin Foon Mark of the Praying Mantis System. Ralph is a world rated kick boxer. He is a dynamic fighter and forms competitor. Ralph kicked me in the head with a hook kick in the 1970's. His amazing speed is his greatest asset. I learned a lot from watching Ralph perform. He was my sparring partner in the 1970's. He is a legend in kungfu circles. A real black man with fantastic martial skills. After a tour of duty in Vietnam, he trained with Thai-Boxers in Thailand and won his division in the Second World Kuoshu Tournament in the Republic of China. Presently, he is studying Vee Jitsu with Prof. Florendo Visitacion. He developed the Universal Defense System, which is representative of the interdisciplinary cross training that make up his many years of experience. Ralph still prefers to consider himself a professional student, always seeking to learn.

CHAPTER FOUR

THE CHAMPIONS

The champions are a unique breed of martial artists. Most students of the martial arts never enter competition. Competition is not for everyone. When you enter the arena of competition, many variables come into play. There is politics, unqualified judges and referee's, and good old cheating. I competed for over thirty years in sparring, kata, weapons and self defense categories. During my years of competition, I had the honor of meeting many of the champions in the ring. The essence of competition is to get better and better. Winning and losing develop better skills. You have to lose in order to win. Every champion has lost more than they ever win. It is the process of elimination. The elimination of bad skills, replaced by good skills. There are local, national and international champions. The two areas of combat are point matches and full contact matches. Until the mid-1960's, only point matches existed in America. Full contact has always been a part of oriental arts.

RON VAN CLIEF AT THE
WORLD CHAMPIONSHIPS
IN HONG KONG (1982)

RON VAN CLIEF
ULTIMATE FIGHTING
CHAMPIONSHIP IV, 1994

In the mid 1960's, the hybrid called full contact karate was born in America. The PKA, WPKO, WUKO,WAKO, WFC and many other organizations were born. Many of the great champions are not at all interested in tournaments. There is just too much politics in the martial arts. We cannot confuse tournament fighting with real fighting. They are two different areas of expertise. Point tournaments are like a game of tag. Contact fighting, sometimes called full contact, is a misnomer. It should be called contact karate. Full contact in the orient is no holds barred. Knees and elbows are allowed. Tournaments should be strictly on the amateur level. So called professionalism in the martial arts will create a hybrid, like professional wrestling. More hype than the real thing. It is nice to see that one can make a living from the martial arts. It is my opinion that the AAU should control the martial arts. Professional martial artists should get paid just like professional boxers.

On December 16, 1994, I had the honor of fighting in the Ultimate Fighting Championship. The UFC is the first professional, mixed match event in America. The Ultimate Fighting Championship is the ultimate! In 1995, I was appointed IFC Commissioner. The IFC is the governing body of the Ultimate Fighting Championship. Cross training is the secret of successful competing.

The martial arts have come a long way, and have a long way to go. The champions are the core of real dedicated martial artists. To become a champion, it takes dedication and discipline. Having competed for over three decades, I have seen the transition that the martial arts have made in America. Martial arts competitors are the gladiators of today. These are the champions of the martial arts today.

SHIHAN WILLIAM OLIVER

Shihan William Oliver is a three time All American Champion, a great fighter and kata competitor. He has fought in the Kyokushinkai World Championships in Japan, and was the star of *Fighting Black Kings,* a documentary of the black martial arts experience in Japan. His leg techniques are truly incredible. He is a student and teacher of Seido Karate and disciple of Grandmaster Tadashi Nakamura. One of the best fighters of the 1960's and 1970's, his speed and flexibility are legendary in the sport karate world.

ABOVE / RIGHT:

WILLIAM OLIVER

MASTER SHELDON WILKINS

Master Sheldon Wilkins has studied the martial arts for over twenty years. He is a former East Coast and New York State Champion, dedicated to true martial arts competition. He had the ability to escape and evade even the best fighters. His unique form of karate and gung fu has mesmerized audiences around the world. Sheldon's warm demeanor disguised his combative techniques. He used the element of surprise to win many of his matches. Sheldon would make you chase him until he caught you. Grandmaster Peter Urban calls him the Magician.

SIFU WILLIE "BAM" JOHNSON

Sifu Johnson is a master of Chinese Kung fu. He has studied various forms of martial arts for over 20 years. A national competitor with a long list of credits. His self defense is really unique and exciting. Weapons and forms are his specialties. He is a black man with a real sense of reality. He travels nationally, demonstrating his unique form of Afro-Chinese martial arts. Willie will soon be appearing in a feature film with Tom Berenger.

ABOVE:

WILLIE JOHNSON

55

MASTER GLORIA DUBISSETTE

ABOVE:

GLORIA DUBISSETTE,
FIGHTING STANCE

RIGHT:

FRONT KICK

Master DuBissette has been a student of the martial arts for over 20 years. She is an excellent fighter and forms competitor. I have personally known Gloria for over 15 years. We sparred many times. She holds the rank of 4th Degree Black Belt in the Chinese Goju System and is presently living and teaching in Washington, D. C. at the YMCA and YWCA. She also teaches at the Women's Crisis Center. Gloria holds black belts in Tae Kwon Do, Arnis and Aikijitsu. She believes that every woman should have basic self defense skills.

MASTER STEVE "NASTY" ANDERSON

Nasty Anderson is a dynamic fighter. He held the championship longer than anyone in sport karate. He is a member of the Black Belt Hall of Fame. Master Anderson is a legend in sport karate. Watching Nasty Anderson and Billy Blanks fight was something to behold. His flying back fist was dazzling. I am proud that I have had the honor to have known him. He has all the right attributes, height, power, speed and tactical strategy. A real gentleman and credit to the martial arts, his records will probably never be broken.

ABOVE:

STEVE ANDERSON

ABOVE / RIGHT / FACING PAGE:

BILLY BLANKS

MASTER BILLY BLANKS

Master Billy Blanks is a fantastic fighter and teacher of Tae Kwon Do. I have known Billy for over twenty-five years. He is a six time World Champion and 10 time United States Champion. In one word he is awesome. During our sparring sessions together, many techniques passed between us. He is almost unstoppable on the outside. His legs are awesome. Billy can kick from any angle, moving forward or backward. Whenever I am on the west coast, I train with Billy. Presently, Billy has starred in over twenty feature action films. This is a great way for Billy to showcase his amazing skills. In the film, *King of the Kickboxers*, Billy jumps into the air and executes three different kicks before landing. That was an incredible sequence. The World Karate Center in Sherman Oaks, California is where you can find him working in the gym or the dojo. You can be sure he will be working. I thought I was the only teacher that taught the thousand kick per class religion. Billy is in incredible shape and is teacher to the stars in Hollywood, and a member of the Black Belt Hall of Fame. Fighting with Billy is indeed a memorable experience, to say the least. He can execute a flying leg scissors in sparring with ease. I will remember my days on the mat with him as special and enlightening. He is a legend in sport karate. You can't go into a video store any place without seeing several Billy Blanks features on the shelf. Billy has come a long way and there is no stopping him. Stay strong, my brother.

CHAPTER FIVE

THE SCREEN HEROES

SHIDOSHI RON VAN CLIEF

ABOVE:

THE BLACK DRAGON

FACING PAGE:

THE BLACK DRAGON'S
REVENGE (top)

BLACK DRAGON FEVER
(bottom)

I starred as the character, The Black Dragon in seven kung fu films. These films were shot in Hong Kong, the Philippines, Thailand and Korea. The Black Dragon was the first film starring a black man as the hero. *The Black Dragon, The Death of Bruce Lee* a.k.a. *The Black Dragon's Revenge, The Super Weapon, Kung fu Fever, The Black Dragon of Shaolin* and *The Bamboo Trap* are available on video cassette. I started my film career in the late 1960's, working on black exploitation films like *Shaft* and *Across 110 Street*. In 1965, I became a member of the East Coast Stuntmen's Association. This was the year that I won my first karate world championship. In 1973, I attended a casting call. Yangtze Films was looking for a black man to star in a series of kung fu films. Serafim Karalexis, the American co-producer, gave me my start in kung fu action films. Already a world champion, I quickly adapted to choreography and became the Black Dragon. From 1981 to 1995, I wrote several martial arts textbooks, *The Manual of the Martial Arts, The Ron Van Clief White Belt Guidebook, The Ron Van Clief Green* and *Purple Belt Guidebook, The Ron Van Clief Brown Belt Guidebook, The Ron Van Clief Black Belt Guidebook, The Ron Van Clief*

Instructors Guidebook and *The Ron Van Clief Master Instructor Guidebook*. During this period, I worked on over seventy-five feature films in the United States and abroad. In 1993, I moved to the Cayman Islands to concentrate on a screen writing career. While living in the Cayman Islands, I worked as the Chief Instructor to the Royal Cayman Island Police Department at the Police Training Center. I wrote three screenplays in the Cayman Islands, *The Return of the Black Dragon*, *Dive* and *Skinhead*. Some of the features I've worked on include *Batman Forever, Die Hard 3, Boomerang, White Man's Burden, The Last Dragon, Fade to Black* and *The Shadow Conspiracy*. At age 51, I fought in the Ultimate Fighting Championship in Tulsa, Oklahoma. My first round opponent was Royce Gracie, the Brazilian Jiujitsu world champion. The match lasted four minutes. It will always be one of the most exciting experiences of my competition days. Royce is a superb athlete and a real gentleman. The Gracie Jiujitsu System is the premiere form of grappling in the world today. In 1996, I will return to Hong Kong and Thailand to star in the upcoming feature film, *The Return of the Black Dragon*. The Black Dragon can still breathe fire. Long live the Black Dragon.

MASTER WESLEY SNIPES

Wesley Snipes has become an international star because of his acting and athletic prowess. Trained in Shotokan Karate, Kenpo Karate, Capoeira, Jiujitsu and Chinese Goju. He started his training in Brooklyn, New York. Wesley trained with Master Jeff Ward and Sensei Marcus Salgado. Presently, he is studying with Grandmaster Steve Muhammad. Watching his fight scenes in *Demolition Man, New Jack City* and *The Money Train,* were testaments of his martial arts proficiency. Bruce Lee told me that Steve Muhammad had the fastest hands he had ever seen. I had the opportunity to visit Wesley and Steve in their camper on the set of *Money Train.* Wesley looked in extremely good shape, mentally and physically. We talked about the old days and the Ultimate Fighting Championship. They expressed an interest in grappling techniques. It was my honor and pleasure to have been in the company of Grandmaster Muhammad. Steve is a true Afro-American Grandmaster of the highest order. I am very proud of you my brothers. Growing up in a ghetto environment did not stop Wesley from becoming a major motion picture star. As Grandmaster Moses Powell always said to me, "watch your back!" Stay healthy and strong.

KYOSHI TAIMAK, THE LAST DRAGON

LEFT / ABOVE:

TAIMAK

Taimak started his training with Master Gerald Orange when he was 6 years old. Gerald Orange was a senior black belt with my Aiki mentor, Grandmaster Peter Urban, 10th degree Red Belt. Grandmaster Urban taught me the essence of Aikijitsu and Goju karate. Taimak has trained with me since the mid 1970's. He is my number one student. Having trained with me for over two decades, Taimak is my martial arts son. My son, Ron Jr., calls Taimak his older brother. Taimak told me that Bruce Lee and I were his role models in the martial arts. In 1984, when Mr. Michael Schultz came to me with the screenplay, *The Last Dragon,* I could not think of anyone else for the role. Although they interviewed thousands of martial artists, Taimak won the role. *The Last Dragon* catapulted Taimak to international stardom. In twenty years, Taimak has reached the level of 7th degree Red Belt. Master Taimak is a national champion in karate competition. He has worked on the silver screen with Janet Jackson, Debbie Allen, Lisa Bonet, Vanity, Bill Cosby and many celebrities. He has worked as a personal fitness trainer and security agent for many personalities such as Mike Tyson and George Benson. Presently living in Los Angeles, Taimak recently completed *Take Control* with Taimak, a self defense workout video for home study. He is a positive role model for the black youth. I am proud to have had Taimak as my student and friend. At thirty years old, he is the youngest Red Belt in the world. He will continue to be an inspiration to the youth all over the world.

JIM KELLY

Jim Kelly is a former Kenpo karate champion that rose to international stardom when Bruce Lee selected him to co-star in the film epic, *Enter the Dragon*. He went on to star in many action films that highlighted his martial arts skills. *Black Belt Jones, The Black Samurai, Three The Hard Way, Take a Hard Ride* and *Hot Potato,* are just a few of his films. I met Jim in Hong Kong in the 1970's. We performed together in Chicago at the Tournament of the Century. Jim Kelly is a Kenpo stylist that combined his own unique form of karate and acting to be a positive role model for many youths throughout the world. My favorite film was *Black Belt Jones.* Gloria Hendry co-starred with Jim and demonstrated some excellent karate techniques.

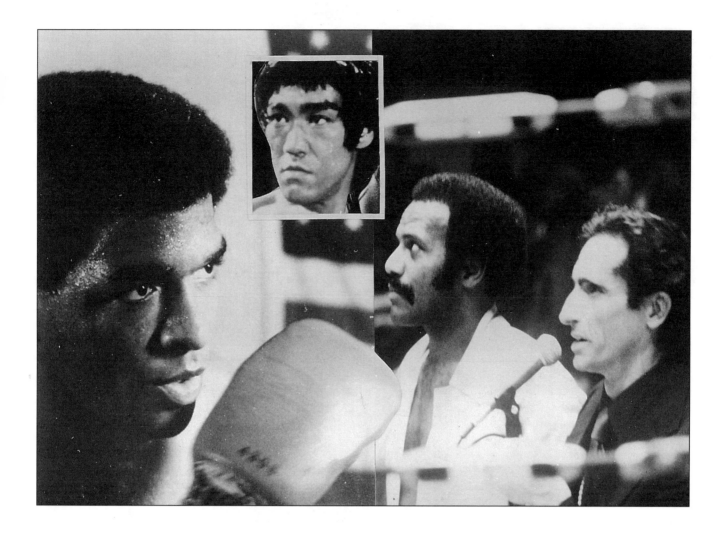

FRED WILLIAMSON

F red "The Hammer" Williamson is a former professional football player, and a fifth degree black belt in the Goju style, under Grandmaster Aaron Banks. He achieved his black belt in the mid 1970's. An action star of the highest caliber, Fred has become internationally know for his physical prowess. I met Fred in the 1970's, at the Oriental World of Self Defense at Madison Square Garden in New York City. He has contributed to the martial arts by displaying his karate techniques in many of his feature films. I am proud to have known him. We worked together on the feature film, *Fist of Fear, Touch of Death*. Fred has become a fine director and producer of what was termed black exploitation films of the 1970's. *Three the Hard Way* and *Buck Town* were two of his most memorable screen performances. Fred's unique style of acting and directing combines humor with outstanding action sequences. Fred has been an inspiration to millions of black youths throughout the world.

MASTER EARNEST HART, JR.

Earnest Hart, Jr. is the only man to ever win four World Kickboxing titles in the Welterweight class. He is recognized as holding black belt or expert rank in 15 different styles of martial arts. Master Hart is a ninth degree black belt. He is the director and founder of the American Fighting Arts School of Martial Arts. In 30 years of martial arts study, he has competed all over the world. He has appeared in and served as technical consultant on Hollywood films, including *Karate Kid III, To Live and Die in L. A., Shootfighter* and *Mortal Kombat. Inside Karate* magazine has named Earnest one of the top ten kickboxers of all time. I have known Earnest for over 20 years. He is an incredible competitor, Sensei, and martial arts referee. Presently, he is the Judge of the Ultimate Fighting Championship. Master Hart lives in St. Louis, Missouri with his wife Marcy, their daughter Grace, and son Trey.

CHAPTER SIX

THE BLACK HEROES OF THE MARTIAL ARTS 1965 – 1995

DRAWING OF CHAKA ZULU BY
MAESTRO ANGEL IBANEZ

OVERLEAF:

THE GOLDEN SWAN

HUI CAMBRELEN
"EL TIGRE NEGRO"

1965

BEST FIGHTER *Tom LaPuppet*

BEST KATA *Chaka Zulu*

BEST WEAPONS *Ronald Moore a.k.a. Taganashi*

BEST DEMONSTRATION *Ron Van Clief*

TEACHER OF THE YEAR *Moses Powell*

MARTIAL ARTS AUTHOR *Fred Hamilton*

MARTIAL ARTS SUPERSTAR *Steve Muhammad*

PIONEER OF THE YEAR *George Cofield*

HALL OF FAME *Jimmy Jones and Mfudishi Maasi*

HONORABLE MENTION *Fred Miller, Rene Gaines,*
Finlay Townsend, Karriem Allah and Earl Monroe

1966

BEST FIGHTER *Tom LaPuppet*

BEST KATA *Steve Muhammad*

BEST WEAPONS *Chaka Zulu*

BEST DEMONSTRATION *Tong Dojo*

TEACHER OF THE YEAR *George Cofield*

MARTIAL ARTS AUTHOR *Ron Taganashi*

MARTIAL ARTS SUPERSTAR *Hawk Frazier*

PIONEER OF THE YEAR *Ronald Duncan*

HALL OF FAME *Leon Wallace*

HONORABLE MENTION *Monroe Marrow, Fred Miller,*
Preston Carter, Skipper Ingham and Howard Jackson

GLEN PERRY AND RON VAN CLIEF

THE BLACK DRAGON IN HONG KONG KICKBOXING MATCH

1967

BEST FIGHTER *Owen Watson*

BEST KATA *Fred Miller*

BEST WEAPONS *George Crayton*

BEST DEMONSTRATION *Chaka Zulu*

TEACHER OF THE YEAR *Tom LaPuppet*

MARTIAL ARTS AUTHOR *Preston Carter*

MARTIAL ARTS SUPERSTAR *Teddy Wilson*

PIONEER OF THE YEAR *Fred Hamilton*

HALL OF FAME *Gerald Orange*

HONORABLE MENTION *Errol Bennet, Billy Davis, Joe Hayes, Richie Havens and Booty Neal*

1968

BEST FIGHTER *Fred Miller*

BEST KATA *Errol Bennet*

BEST WEAPONS *Tayari Casel*

BEST DEMONSTRATION *John Davis*

TEACHER OF THE YEAR *Karriem Allah*

MARTIAL ARTS AUTHOR *Tom LaPuppet*

MARTIAL ARTS SUPERSTAR *Steve Muhammad*

PIONEER OF THE YEAR *Ron Austin*

HALL OF FAME *Victor Moore*

HONORABLE MENTION *Earl Monroe, Albert Cheeks, Speedy Leacock, Little K. A., Calvin Wilder and Papasan Canty*

BILLY BLANKS

DONNIE COLLINS IN ACTION

1969

BEST FIGHTER *Ron Van Clief*

BEST KATA *Errol Bennet*

BEST WEAPONS *Jimmy Jones*

BEST DEMONSTRATION *Donnie Williams*

TEACHER OF THE YEAR *Mfudishi Maasi*

MARTIAL ARTS AUTHOR *George Cofield*

MARTIAL ARTS SUPERSTAR *Curtis Faust*

PIONEER OF THE YEAR *Isaac Henry*

HALL OF FAME *George Binns*

HONORABLE MENTION *Owen Watson, Earl Thompson, Earl Monroe, Teddy Wilson and Hawk Frazier*

OWEN WATSON

1970

BEST FIGHTER *Ron Van Clief*

BEST KATA *William Oliver*

BEST WEAPONS *Ronald Duncan*

BEST DEMONSTRATION *Moses Powell*

TEACHER OF THE YEAR *Karriem Allah*

MARTIAL ARTS AUTHOR *Tom LaPuppet*

MARTIAL ARTS SUPERSTAR *Jim Kelly*

PIONEER OF THE YEAR *Fred Hamilton*

HALL OF FAME *Earl Monroe and Skipper Ingham*

HONORABLE MENTION *Mike Warren, Earnest Hart Jr., Little John Davis, Howard Jackson and Tayari Casel*

CHEREMA STOKER

1971

BEST FIGHTER *Errol Bennet*

BEST KATA *William Oliver*

BEST WEAPONS *Tayari Casel*

BEST DEMONSTRATION *Nisei Goju*

TEACHER OF THE YEAR *Isaac Henry Jr.*

MARTIAL ARTS AUTHOR *Jimmy Jones*

MARTIAL ARTS SUPERSTAR *Jim Kelly*

PIONEER OF THE YEAR *Ron Austin*

HALL OF FAME *Preston Carter*

HONORABLE MENTION *Steve Saunders, Sam Roberts,*
Billy Blanks, Howard Jackson and Donnie Collins

1972

BEST FIGHTER *Ron Van Clief*

BEST KATA *Tayari Casel*

BEST WEAPONS *Ron Van Clief*

BEST DEMONSTRATION *Chaka Zulu*

TEACHER OF THE YEAR *Moses Powell*

MARTIAL ARTS AUTHOR *Karriem Allah*

MARTIAL ARTS SUPERSTAR *Donnie Williams*

PIONEER OF THE YEAR *Billy Davis*

HALL OF FAME *Tom LaPuppet*

HONORABLE MENTION *Earl Thompson, Fred Miller,*
Monroe Marrow, Howard Jackson and Aaron Pryor

FUTURE HEROES

RICHIE HAVENS

1973

BEST FIGHTER *Hawk Frazier*

BEST KATA *Little John Davis*

BEST WEAPONS *Ernest Hyman*

BEST DEMONSTRATION *Ron Jeter*

TEACHER OF THE YEAR *Ronald Duncan*

MARTIAL ARTS AUTHOR *Kalai Griffin*

MARTIAL ARTS SUPERSTAR *Richie Havens*

PIONEER OF THE YEAR *Maynard Miner*

HALL OF FAME *Ron Austin*

HONORABLE MENTION *Lamar Thornton, Speedy Leacock, Tom Ervin, Herbie Thompson and Bradford Gonzales*

1974

BEST FIGHTER *Little John Davis*

BEST KATA *Errol Bennet*

BEST WEAPONS *Robert Crosson*

BEST DEMONSTRATION *Owen Watson*

TEACHER OF THE YEAR *Monroe Marrow*

MARTIAL ARTS AUTHOR *Preston Carter*

MARTIAL ARTS SUPERSTAR *Ron Van Clief*

PIONEER OF THE YEAR *Leon Wallace*

HALL OF FAME *Skipper Ingham*

HONORABLE MENTION *Donnie Collins, Owen Watson, Harry Morton, Ron Scott, Glen Perry and Tom Ervin*

RENE GAINES

1975

BEST FIGHTER *Ron Van Clief*

BEST KATA *William Oliver*

BEST WEAPONS *Ronald Taganashi*

BEST DEMONSTRATION *Glen Perry*

TEACHER OF THE YEAR *Maynard Minor*

MARTIAL ARTS AUTHOR *Steve Muhammad*

MARTIAL ARTS SUPERSTAR *Gregory Hines*

PIONEER OF THE YEAR *Fred Hamilton and Leon Wallace*

HALL OF FAME *Linda Denley and Joe Hayes*

HONORABLE MENTION *Ron Austin, Robert Crosson, Hawk Frazer, Monroe Marrow, David Washington, Sekwii Sha and Tayari Casel*

RON SCOTT BREAKING A CINDER BLOCK

RON VAN CLIEF, 1969 WORLD CHAMPIONSHIPS

1976

BEST FIGHTER *Earl Monroe*

BEST KATA *Tayari Casel*

BEST WEAPONS *Little John Davis*

BEST DEMONSTRATION *Karriem Allah*

TEACHER OF THE YEAR *Jonathan Stewart*

MARTIAL ARTS AUTHOR *Bill Hayes*

MARTIAL ARTS SUPERSTAR *Fred Williamson*

PIONEER OF THE YEAR *Donnie Williams*

HALL OF FAME *Howard Jackson*

HONORABLE MENTION *Khemfoia Padu, Sekwii Sha, John Dinkins, Joe Hayes, Ernest Hyman and Little K. A.*

1977

BEST FIGHTER *Joe Hayes*

BEST KATA *William Oliver*

BEST WEAPONS *Claude Battle*

BEST DEMONSTRATION *Seitu Jimmy Dyson*

TEACHER OF THE YEAR *Owen Watson*

MARTIAL ARTS AUTHOR *George Cofield*

MARTIAL ARTS SUPERSTAR *William Oliver*

PIONEER OF THE YEAR *Sekwii Sha*

HALL OF FAME *Earnest Hart Jr.*

HONORABLE MENTION *Chaka Zulu, Abdul Mutakabir,
   Steve Saunders, Donnie Williams and Donnie Collins*

BLACK DRAGON WHITE SNAKE STRIKE

RON VAN CLIEF IN HONG KONG

1978

BEST FIGHTER *Mike Warren*

BEST KATA *Errol Bennet*

BEST WEAPONS *Robert Crosson*

BEST DEMONSTRATION *Moses Powell*

TEACHER OF THE YEAR *Rashon Kahn*

MARTIAL ARTS AUTHOR *Ron Austin*

MARTIAL ARTS SUPERSTAR *Owen Watson*

PIONEER OF THE YEAR *Tommy Agero*

HALL OF FAME *Owen Watson*

HONORABLE MENTION *John Dinkins, Kirk Wood,
   Finlay Townsend, Jim Dyson, Claude Battle,
   Charles Martin and William Oliver*

OBOSAN OWEN WATSON

1979

BEST FIGHTER *Linda Denley*
BEST KATA *Sheldon Wilkins*
BEST WEAPONS *Gerald Orange*
BEST DEMONSTRATION *Ronald Duncan*
TEACHER OF THE YEAR *Malachi Lee*
MARTIAL ARTS AUTHOR *Fred Hamilton*
MARTIAL ARTS SUPERSTAR *Ron Van Clief*
PIONEER OF THE YEAR *Tom LaPuppet*
HALL OF FAME *Donnie Williams*
HONORABLE MENTION *Donnie Collins, Earl Monroe,*
    Danny Gwira, Errol Bennet and Chaka Zulu

1980

BEST FIGHTER *William Oliver*
BEST KATA *Errol Bennet*
BEST WEAPONS *Rico Guy*
BEST DEMONSTRATION *Willie Johnson*
TEACHER OF THE YEAR *Ron Austin*
MARTIAL ARTS AUTHOR *Ron Van Clief*
MARTIAL ARTS SUPERSTAR *Billy Blanks*
PIONEER OF THE YEAR *Owen Watson*
HALL OF FAME *Don Jacob and Errol Lynn*
HONORABLE MENTION *Teddy Wilson,*
    Ron Scott, Victor Moore, Howard Jackson
    and David Washington

Photo: Ms. Desepe Thomson

TAYARI CASEL

THE BLACK DRAGON IN THE PHILIPPINES

1981

BEST FIGHTER *Billy Blanks*

BEST KATA *William Oliver*

BEST WEAPONS *Little John Davis*

BEST DEMONSTRATION *Robert Crosson*

TEACHER OF THE YEAR *Errol Bennet*

MARTIAL ARTS AUTHOR *Ron Van Clief*

MARTIAL ARTS SUPERSTAR *Carl Scott*

PIONEER OF THE YEAR *Steve Muhammad*

HALL OF FAME *Fred Miller*

HONORABLE MENTION *Ron Van Clief Jr.,*
   Taimak, Dorria Ameen, Billy Davis
   and Sekwii Sha

1982

BEST FIGHTER *Steve Anderson*

BEST KATA *Willie "Bam" Johnson*

BEST WEAPONS *Taimak*

BEST DEMONSTRATION *Ron Van Clief Jr.*

TEACHER OF THE YEAR *Steve Muhammad*

MARTIAL ARTS AUTHOR *Don Jacob*

MARTIAL ARTS SUPERSTAR *Fred Williamson*

PIONEER OF THE YEAR *Billy Davis*

HALL OF FAME *Little John Davis*

HONORABLE MENTION *Richard Sinclair,*
   Everett Eddy, Finlay Townsend, Gerald
   Orange and Errol Bennet

RON VAN CLIEF AND CONAN LEE IN HONG
KONG FREEFIGHTING CHAMPIONSHIP

THE BLACK DRAGON AND DRAGON LEE

1983

BEST FIGHTER *Earnest Hart Jr.*

BEST KATA *William Oliver*

BEST WEAPONS *Torrance Mathis*

BEST DEMONSTRATION *Ron Jeter*

TEACHER OF THE YEAR *Ron Van Clief*

MARTIAL ARTS AUTHOR *Curtis Faust*

MARTIAL ARTS SUPERSTAR *Jim Kelly*

PIONEER OF THE YEAR *Billy Blanks*

HALL OF FAME *Jimmy Jones*

HONORABLE MENTION *Ben Peacock,
Otis Baker, Preston Baker, Linda Denley
and Shorty Mills*

1984

BEST FIGHTER *Donnie Collins*

BEST KATA *William Oliver*

BEST WEAPONS *Frank Hargrove*

BEST DEMONSTRATION *Chaka Zulu*

TEACHER OF THE YEAR *George Cofield*

MARTIAL ARTS AUTHOR *Jimmy Jones*

MARTIAL ARTS SUPERSTAR *Sheldon Wilkins*

PIONEER OF THE YEAR *Moses Powell*

HALL OF FAME *Linda Denley*

HONORABLE MENTION *Cherema Stoker, Rene
Gaines, Gloria DuBissette and Dorria Ameen*

KUNG FU FEVER

1985

BEST FIGHTER *Billy Blanks*

BEST KATA *Kevin Thompson*

BEST WEAPONS *Jeff Ward*

BEST DEMONSTRATION *Ron Van Clief*

TEACHER OF THE YEAR *Tom LaPuppet*

MARTIAL ARTS AUTHOR *Ron Van Clief*

MARTIAL ARTS SUPERSTAR *Taimak*

PIONEER OF THE YEAR *Linda Denley*

HALL OF FAME *Ronald Duncan*

HONORABLE MENTION *Ron Van Clief Jr.,
Kalai Griffin, Elsworth Grant, Rico Guy,
Earl Monroe and Geddes Hislop*

THE BLACK DRAGON'S REVENGE

THE DEATH OF BRUCE LEE

1986

BEST FIGHTER *Steve "Nasty" Anderson*

BEST KATA *Derek Williams*

BEST WEAPONS *Willie "Bam" Johnson*

BEST DEMONSTRATION *Ronald Duncan*

TEACHER OF THE YEAR *Dennis Brown*

MARTIAL ARTS AUTHOR *Skipper Ingham*

MARTIAL ARTS SUPERSTAR *Billy Blanks*

PIONEER OF THE YEAR *Billy Davis*

HALL OF FAME *Ralph Mitchell*

HONORABLE MENTION *Haisan Kaleak,
Herbie Kerr, Billy T. Taylor,
Julius Carey and Jeff Ward*

THE BLACK DRAGON AT THE SHAOLIN TEMPLE

1987

BEST FIGHTER *Ralph Mitchell*

BEST KATA *Kevin Thompson*

BEST WEAPONS *Haisan Kaleak*

BEST DEMONSTRATION *George Crayton*

TEACHER OF THE YEAR *Jonathan Stewart*

MARTIAL ARTS AUTHOR *Jonathan Stewart*

MARTIAL ARTS SUPERSTAR *Howard Jackson*

PIONEER OF THE YEAR *Jesse Glover*

HALL OF FAME *Little John Davis*

HONORABLE MENTION *Linda Ranson, Dennis Brown, David James, Richard Sinclair and Gerald Orange*

1988

BEST FIGHTER *Ron Van Clief*

BEST KATA *Skipper Ingham*

BEST WEAPONS *Doug Pierre*

BEST DEMONSTRATION *Ron Van Clief*

TEACHER OF THE YEAR *Chaka Zulu*

MARTIAL ARTS AUTHOR *Owen Watson*

MARTIAL ARTS SUPERSTAR *William Oliver*

PIONEER OF THE YEAR *Ron Jeter*

HALL OF FAME *Linda Denley*

HONORABLE MENTION *Mike Kelly, Oak Tree Edwards, Richard Joiner, Monster Man Eddy and Errol Bennet*

THE BLACK DRAGON'S REVENGE

THE BLACK DRAGON'S REVENGE

1989

BEST FIGHTER *Ron Van Clief*

BEST KATA *William Oliver*

BEST WEAPONS *Haisan Kaleak*

BEST DEMONSTRATION *George Crayton*

TEACHER OF THE YEAR *Errol Bennet*

MARTIAL ARTS AUTHOR *Rico Guy*

MARTIAL ARTS SUPERSTAR *Jim Kelly*

PIONEER OF THE YEAR *Mfudishi Maasi*

HALL OF FAME *Little John Davis*

HONORABLE MENTION *Willie Johnson,
Taimak, Ron Van Clief Jr., Doug Pierre,
Arnold LaCruise and Lamar Thornton*

1990

BEST FIGHTER *Taimak*

BEST KATA *Kevin Thompson*

BEST WEAPONS *Haisan Kaleak*

BEST DEMONSTRATION *Little John Davis*

TEACHER OF THE YEAR *Moses Powell*

MARTIAL ARTS AUTHOR *Don Jacob*

MARTIAL ARTS SUPERSTAR *Billy Blanks*

PIONEER OF THE YEAR *Ron Van Clief*

HALL OF FAME *Jonathan Stewart and George Binns*

HONORABLE MENTION *Rashon Kahn, Ivor Archie,
George Crayton, Robert Lewis,
Michael Holmes and Geddes Hislop*

THE BLACK DRAGON AT THE WORLD CHAMPIONSHIPS
IN HONG KONG, 1982

THE BLACK DRAGON ON LOCATION

1991

BEST FIGHTER *Mafia Holloway*

BEST KATA *Kevin Thompson*

BEST WEAPONS *Chaka Zulu*

BEST DEMONSTRATION *Taimak*

TEACHER OF THE YEAR *Herbie Thompson*

MARTIAL ARTS AUTHOR *Donnie Williams*

MARTIAL ARTS SUPERSTAR *Steve James*

PIONEER OF THE YEAR *Don Jacob*

HALL OF FAME *Steve "Nasty" Anderson*

HONORABLE MENTION *David James,*
   Doug Pierre, Ed Primus, Caroline
   Primus and Janet Bloem

1992

BEST FIGHTER *Kevin Thompson*

BEST KATA *Derrick Williams*

BEST WEAPONS *Taimak*

BEST DEMONSTRATION *Ron Van Clief*

TEACHER OF THE YEAR *David Washington*

MARTIAL ARTS AUTHOR *Richard Sinclair*

MARTIAL ARTS SUPERSTAR *Wesley Snipes*

PIONEER OF THE YEAR *Billy Blanks*

HALL OF FAME *George Binns*

HONORABLE MENTION *Garth Binns, Gilbert*
McLean, Michael Holmes, Claude Myles,
Terry Bradshaw and Robert Lewis

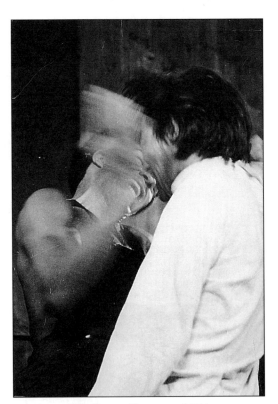

THE BLACK DRAGON, 1974
MANILA, PHILIPPINES

THE NEW TERRITORIES, HONG KONG, 1974

1993

BEST FIGHTER *Steve "Nasty" Anderson*

BEST KATA *Derrick Williams*

BEST WEAPONS *Doug Pierre*

BEST DEMONSTRATION *Glen Perry*

TEACHER OF THE YEAR *Taimak*

MARTIAL ARTS AUTHOR *Chaka Zulu*

MARTIAL ARTS SUPERSTAR *Steve James*

PIONEER OF THE YEAR *Tom LaPuppet*

HALL OF FAME *Billy Blanks*

HONORABLE MENTION *Chief Inspector Dixon, Ivor Archie, Keith Dixon, Daoud Tyler-Ameen, Elsworth Grant, Art Jimmerson, Pat Smith and Cherry Chin*

1994

BEST FIGHTER *Peter "Sugarfoot" Cunningham*

BEST KATA *Derrick Williams*

BEST WEAPONS *David James*

BEST DEMONSTRATIONS *Ron Van Clief*

TEACHER OF THE YEAR *Karriem Ali Abdul Jabbar*

MARTIAL ARTS AUTHOR *Ron Van Clief*

MARTIAL ARTS SUPERSTAR *Wesley Snipes*

PIONEER OF THE YEAR *Chaka Zulu*

HALL OF FAME *Steve James and Jesse Glover*

HONORABLE MENTION *Lascelles Johnson, Virginia Johnson, Julius Carey, Doug Pierre, Esteban Van Clief, Orlando Weit, Johnny Rhodes, Felix Lee Mitchell, Pat Smith, Ron Van Clief, Marcus Bossett, Larry Cureton and Melton Bowen*

THE BLACK DRAGON IN MANILA, 1974

Photo: Nilsa LaSalle

THE BLACK DRAGON, 1996

1995

BEST FIGHTER *Pedro Xavier*

BEST KATA *Derrick Williams*

BEST WEAPONS *Willy "The Bam" Johnson*

BEST DEMONSTRATION *Hakim Alston*

TEACHER OF THE YEAR *Tom LaPuppet*

MARTIAL ARTS AUTHOR *Ron Van Clief*

MARTIAL ARTS SUPERSTAR *Wesley Snipes*

PIONEER OF THE YEAR *Steve Muhammad*

HALL OF FAME *Jeff Ward*

HONORABLE MENTION: *Pat Smith, Joe Charles, Gerry Harris and Earnest Hart Jr.*

1995

HALL of FAME MEMBERS

GRANDMASTER
THOMAS LA PUPPET

GRANDMASTER FRED HAMILTON

Grandmaster Hamilton was a master of traditional Shotokan Karate. He studied in Japan in the 1940's. Grandmaster Hamilton brought the martial arts to Harlem in the 1950's. He was the first black karate tournament promoter in America. The All Dojo Tournament was a landmark in New York competition. All the great competitors would come to his tournament. He is responsible for creating full contact karate without gloves, an innovator that created the Karate Olympics, and decathlon events that tested martial artists athletic prowess. His tournaments were legendary in the New York area. Grandmaster Hamilton created his unique form of Afro-American karate for his people. A nationalist, author, community activist, veteran and dedicated father. Grandmaster Hamilton will surely be missed by his many students and the martial arts community. Old masters never die, their legends live on forever.

GRANDMASTER STEVE MUHAMMAD

Grandmaster Muhammad aka Saunders is a legend in the world of the martial arts. Bruce Lee told me that Steve had the fastest hands he had ever seen. He is a great competitor, who has taught Kenpo Karate for over thirty years. A student of Grandmaster Ed Parker of Pasadena, California, Master Muhammad is the founder of the Black Karate Federation. He is a policeman who works with gang violence in Los Angeles, an international Grand Champion, and pillar of the martial arts community. He has performed in numerous films from *Enter the Dragon* to the *Karate Kid*. A member of the Black Belt Hall of Fame and recipient of the Martial Arts Lifetime Achievement Award, he is a great man and a fantastic martial artist. Steve is currently the trainer and bodyguard of superstar Wesley Snipes.

GRANDMASTER DON JACOB

Prof. Don Jacob is the founder of the Purple Dragon System of martial arts. Don-jitsu-ryu is an eclectic style of self defense that encompasses many different forms of martial arts. His self defense is awesome to watch. He is a former student of Grandmaster Moses Powell, in the early days. A member of the Martial Arts Hall of Fame, he is responsible for bringing jiu-jitsu to Trinidad and the West Indies. He has established the Purple Dragon Don Jitsu-ryu system all over the world. I am proud to know such a great master, a proud black man who knows his African roots. Prof. Jacob has written several textbooks on the Purple Dragon System that are available internationally.

GRANDMASTER RON MOORE AKA TAGANASHI

Grandmaster Taganashi was the co-founder of Nisei Goju. He was a 10th degree Red Belt. A master of Ninjitsu, Japanese Goju Karate, Kendo, Iaido, Tai Chi, Kung fu and Weaponry. Sensei Taganashi taught me how to do 1000 Side Kicks. An ex-marine, he was expert in Sparring, Kata and Weaponry. Grandmaster Taganashi died physically, but he will always be remembered in martial arts folklore. Great martial artists like Ron dedicated their whole lives to the study of the martial arts. I am proud to say that he was my teacher. He was also a Zen master and a member of the native American community. For over thirty years, he was a pillar of the world martial arts community. He was a national champion in sparring, kata and fighting, and a member of the Martial Arts Hall of Fame and the Masters in Action Hall of Fame.

MASTER KAREEM ALI ABDUL JABBAR

Master Jabbar began his training under Grandmaster Koang Woong Kim in 1974. With the help of Grandmaster Kim, Abdul-Jabbar has won a number of titles including National Champion, and countless open championships. The transition from athlete to teacher has been a smooth one for Master Abdul-Jabbar. He is a member of the board of Governors and Athletes Advisory Counsel of the United States Tae Kwon Do Union. He holds the rank of 6th degree Black Belt. His educational accomplishments include a Bachelors of Science Degree in Physical Education, certified to teach grades Kindergarten thru twelve, and a Masters of Science Degree in Kinesiology/Exercise. Presently, he operates the Cayman Island Tae Kwon Do Training Center. His team represented the Cayman Islands in the 1994 Tae Kwon Do World Games.

SIJO GEORGE CRAYTON JR.

Sijo Crayton has taught his eclectic Afro-American style of Kung fu, Looang Foo Pai (Dragon Tiger Style) for over 20 years. His kwoon in Queens, New York, has produced many local and national champions. George is an excellent forms competitor of the highest caliber. In the 1960's and 1970's, he reigned in forms competition. A real showman capable of getting an audience up on their feet. I have known George for over twenty-five years and respect him highly.

MASTER HAISAN KALEAK

Soke Haisan Kaleak is a member of the World Martial Arts Hall of Fame. He is a student of Grandmaster Moses Powell for two decades. He is a national weapons competitor with many awards and trophies. His Bow Staff form is incredibly beautiful to watch. Haisan is a master of Jiu-jitsu self defense.

SHIHAN DAVID JAMES

Shihan James is a master of Vee-jitsu and Arnis, a student of Prof. Florendo Visitacion, the mentor of legendary Moses Powell. Shihan James is an expert in weaponry. The knife and stick are his specialties. Watching him do knife technique is truly enlightening. He is a member of the World Martial Arts Hall of Fame.

PETER "SUGARFOOT" CUNNINGHAM

Sugarfoot Cunningham is one of the new breed of full contact fighters, a real technician capable of knocking out his opponents with either hand or foot techniques. He is in excellent shape and trains at the world famous Jet Center in Van Nuys, California. Peter is the current W. K. A. World Lightweight Champion. A film career is in the near future.

SIFU TAYARI CASEL

Sifu Casel is a master of Kung fu, Capoeira, Escrima and Arnis. In the early 1970's, he was quite a devastating force of Afro-American presence on the martial arts scene. Tayari would wear African clothing as his martial arts uniform, Kinte cloth hats and belts with black kung fu pants. He was an excellent ground fighter. In the 1970's, he used Capoeira in tournaments. Tayari and I were room mates and dojo brothers. I really enjoyed sparring with him. His speed made interesting enhancements in my performance. He was superb at forms and weaponry, a local and national forms, weapons, and fighting champion. A native of Chicago, he presently lives and teaches in the Washington, D. C. area. A creator of Afro-American kung fu and creator of musical forms, Tayari was the first kung fu practitioner that entered karate tournaments. He was an elusive and effective fighter. Sifu Tayari Casel is a member of the Afro-American Martial Arts Hall of Fame.

MASTER JEFF WARD

Master Ward made his first black belt in the Chinese Goju System under Kyoshi Ron Van Clief and Sensei Sidney Filson, 6th Dan. He went on to study Capoeira, Escrima and Arnis. Jeff started his film career in 1984, in the film, *The Last Dragon*. He was the stunt double for Taimak. Jeff went on to become one of the most famous stunt coordinators in America, working with Denzel Washington, Wesley Snipes and Sylvester Stallone. *Meteor Man, Malcolm X, Mo' Better Blues, Demolition Man, Sugar Hill* and *Ricochet* are some of his long line of film credits He is an excellent choreographer and martial artist. Jeff is a real credit to the black race and the world martial arts community.

SIFU DENNIS BROWN

Sifu Brown is a kung fu practitioner of the highest caliber. Annually, Dennis holds the largest tournament in the Washington, D. C. area. Besides being an excellent competitor, he has traveled to mainland China to study his unique form of Afro-Chinese Kung fu. He and Sifu Tayari Casel were an awesome team. Their spear and sword, two man form was a thing of beauty to watch. Although he has retired from competition, he is a legend in the world of kung fu competitors. Sifu Brown has also traveled to Hong Kong and Taiwan to star in several kung fu feature films.

MASTER JESSE GLOVER

Sifu Glover is the first student that Bruce Lee had when he first came to America. It is interesting that Bruce's first student was a black man. Jesse has continued to work on JKD theories and principles for over twenty years. He is in constant demand for seminars and workshops. He is a member of the World Martial Arts Hall of Fame. Sifu Glover has become a legend in the kung fu world. He is an excellent practitioner and teacher of the martial arts.

MASTER KEVIN THOMPSON

Master Kevin Thompson was called Little K. A. in the 1970's. He is a disciple of the legendary Karriem Allah, a world class athlete and a member of the Transatlantic Oil Team. The Shakil Warrior is an amazing competitor, equally good with hand or foot techniques. Master Thompson is a credit to the art of sport karate. He has traveled internationally competing and demonstrating his awesome skills. He was the 1992 United States Grand Champion. A member of the Black Belt Hall of Fame and the World Karate Hall of Fame. He is an integral part of the new generation of Afro-American martial arts champions. I am proud to say that I have know him for over 20 years. He is absolute proof positive that you can be what you want with hard work.

MASTER LINDA DENLEY

Master Linda Denley is a legend in the world of sport karate. She is truly an awesome fighter. Linda held the United States Championship longer than any woman alive. I have seen her fight many times. She is equally excellent with hand or foot techniques. For over twenty years, she has been the guiding light for women in the martial arts. If I were a woman, I would want to be just like her. Linda's form of Tae Kwon Do, combined with various styles, has made her an awesome competitor. Linda is strong and fast! Her competition records will probably never be broken. Linda Denley is a real black woman warrior and a credit to the world martial arts community. She will always be remembered as a great champion.

MASTER ERROL LYNN

Master Lynn is the head of Seido Karate in Jamaica. He is an excellent fighter, teacher and kata performer. For over twenty years, he has been a driving force for martial arts in the West Indies. Seido Karate is a combination of Shotokan, Goju, Jiujitsu, Judo, Kendo and Weaponry. He produces many local and national champions from his dojo in Kingston, Jamaica. Keep up the good work!

MASTER RICHARD SINCLAIR

Master Sinclair is the founder of the Iron Octopus System of Martial Arts. He is an advisor and author for *Action Arts* magazine. He has studied the martial arts for over thirty years. Master Sinclair is a community minded individual that uses the martial arts as a people builder. He is a member of the World Martial Arts Hall of Fame.

MASTER DERRICK WILLIAMS

Master Williams is a practitioner of the traditional style of Shotokan Karate. An amazing fighter and forms competitor. Watching him perform kata brings visions of the masters of old. A real martial arts scholar of the highest caliber, he has competed for three decades. A local and international champion, that has uncanny precision and spiritual essence, Master Derrick Williams is a modern day samurai.

MASTER ERROL BENNET

Master Bennet is a practitioner of the Shotokan Style of karate. He has studied the martial arts for over 25 years, and is a truly great fighter and kata performer. I have known Errol for over two decades and respect him highly. Master Bennet has taught his unique style of Shotokan, from his dojo in the Bronx. We fought several times in the 1970's. He would always bring the best out of me. Fighting Master Bennet was a great honor for me. I remember losing a match to him by one point at Sunnyside Gardens. It will always be a memorable experience for me. Master Bennet has produced many national and local champions from his Bronx dojo. He is the bodyguard of Diana Ross. She could have not selected a better karate man to be at her side. I will always hold Master Bennet in deepest respect and honor. When I had my dojo in the Bronx in the 1970's, he would come by and spar with me. It was always a great occasion for my students and myself. He is indeed a great man and role model for the black community.

MASTER STEVE JAMES

Master Steve James is a black superstar of the highest order. A student of the martial arts for over 20 years, Steve was a student of Hung Gar, Praying Mantis and Wu Shu. I met Steve in New York in the late 1960's. We were both starving actors. Steve went on to become an international motion picture star. *Delta Force, American Ninja 1 & 2, The Hero and the Terror, Street Hunter and Mantis* were some of his credits. Steve truly is a black hero of the martial arts. Steve was one of the few black men allowed the opportunity to star in Hollywood features. Master Steve James died on Dec. 18, 1993. He was posthumously inducted into the Martial Arts Hall of Fame in 1994.

MASTER HERB KERR

Master Kerr is a student and teacher of Capoeira. Capoeira is a Afro-Brazilian form of martial arts that disguises its self defense movements with dance movements. It is a most fluid form of martial arts. The blend of basic karate, jiujitsu, grappling and throwing movements combined with Afro-Brazilian dance gives Capoeira an almost surrealistic presence. Watching Capoeira practiced is almost hypnotic. Master Herb Kerr started his training in Capoeira almost two decades ago. He has traveled internationally demonstrating his art. In 1984, Herb worked as a stuntman on the feature film, *The Last Dragon*. Master Kerr is an excellent martial artist with a flare for choreography. He is indeed a master of Capoeira and a member of the East Coast Martial Arts Alliance.

MASTER ELSWORTH GRANT

Master Elsworth Grant is the sole Chinese Goju and Aikijitsu representative in the Cayman Islands. He has studied Chinese Goju, Black Dragon Aikijitsu, Wing Tsun, Tai Chi and Ninjitsu weaponry with Shidoshi Ron Van Clief. Over a decade ago, Master Grant started his martial arts education studying Tae Kwon Do, Tang Soo Do and Shotokan karate, Presently, he is a certified teacher, 3rd degree black belt in Chinese Goju, 4th Degree Renshi in Black Dragon Aikijitsu, and certified teacher of Black Dragon Tai Chi. He lives in Grand Cayman and teaches in his West Bay dojo. Keep up the good work!

CHAPTER SEVEN

THE BLACK DRAGON MEMOIRS 1943 – 1996

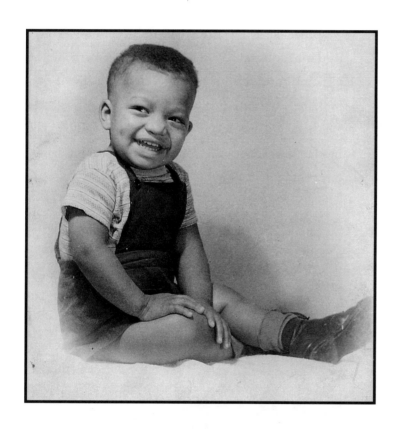

I was born in Brooklyn, New York on January 25, 1943. My only brother, Larry Van Clief, was born on June 9, 1944. We were the son's of Allaire and Doris Van Clief. My brother and I were both born premature, at seven months. My father, Allaire, was a merchant marine and was out to sea when my brother, Larry, and I were born. I was three pounds and nine ounces at birth. My brother was three pounds and twelve ounces. It was hard for a black women alone, with two young children. My father survived being torpedoed in the war by a German submarine. It always seemed as if he was never there for me.

FACING PAGE:

THE BLACK DRAGON, 1981

ABOVE:

RON VAN CLIEF AS A CHILD

My mother is the toughest woman I have ever known. She has always been totally supportive of me, unconditionally. I love my Mom more than anything. Doris was an orphan. She grew up dirt poor. She wore the hand me downs from cousins and nephews. She was given ten cents a day for school. In those days, the bus was five cents in each direction. Normally, she would walk to and from school. Ten cents was a lot in those days. At twelve years old, my mother got her first job. My mother never knew her father. She didn't meet him until she was a grown woman. When I was a teenager, my mother introduced me to bodybuilding. She paid my tuition at a local bodybuilding gym. Kenny Hall, the body-building guru, was my mentor. He taught me the basics of body-building, concentrating on the arms and stomach. Kenny Hall is still bodybuilding at the age of 60 and is in incredible shape. My mother did the very best for the family. She is the best mother anyone could ever have in life.

My only brother, Larry Van Clief, was born on June 9, 1944. He was my father's favorite. We called him Pete because we called my father Larry. We always fought each other. I went into the U. S. Marine Corps in 1960. Larry went into the U. S. Army We wanted to go into the military to escape Brooklyn. Sometimes we would be laying in bed and talk about being soldiers. I was the shy one, but Pete was the brave one. My cousin, Kirk Wood, was his best friend. They were very much alike. Basketball and hanging out was their life. They would play basketball for hours. Of course, they both beat me on the basketball court. Pete and Kirk motivated me to become a good martial artist. I attended Boys High School in Brooklyn, New York. It was the premiere school for athletics in New York.

ABOVE:

RON AND MOTHER, DORIS
CIRCA 1940'S

RIGHT:

RON'S ONLY BROTHER, LARRY
VAN CLIEF, WAS KILLED IN
VIETNAM IN 1966, U. S. ARMY

Connie Hawkins, the pro basketball player, was my classmate. One day, I tied his sneaker laces together. He started to chase me and fell like a giant redwood tree. A few weeks later, he saw me in the gym. I started to run and he threw his sneakers like a bolo at my ankles. I fell right on my face. The great director, Bill Duke attended Boys High School. I will never forget those days with Pete and Kirk in Brooklyn.

Coming from southeast Asia to the subways of New York City was quite a culture shock. I lived in a railroad, walk through apartment on Washington St. and Christopher St., in the West Village. These were truly the days of rock n' roll. During this period, I worked as security for Sly and the Family Stone, The Chambers Brothers, Earth, Wind and Fire, Richie Havens and Jimmy Hendricks. Chaka Zulu hired me to do security at the Electric Circus. The Electric Circus was the premiere night spot of the 1960's, into the 1970's. While working at the Electric Circus, I met black belt Hall of Famer, Tom LaPuppet. We bounced at The Dom.

The Dom was an amazing place. There were so many beautiful women at the Dom. In those days I loved to dance. After graduating from the Transit Police Department I started train patrol. My tour would start at 8 PM and end at 4 AM. These were the peak crime hours in the subway. On the weekends, I worked at the Dom. In those days, many police officers worked other jobs to make ends meet. I worked one year of 8 PM to 4 AM, and two years of 12 Midnight to 8 AM shifts. In 1969, I decided that I would like to concentrate on my martial arts. I resigned from the Transit Police Department in 1969. It actually interfered with my training. I tried to be the best policeman possible. In those days if you were zealous you were not liked. The basic rule was to work as little as possible. I was really gung ho. When you give out tickets and the other cops don't, they look like they are not doing anything. Good cops are discouraged from doing the best they can. My zealousness caused me to be transferred to Coney Island. That's what happens when you are too active. There is a great deal of racism in the police departments of America. I joined the Police Department because I wanted to make a difference.

ABOVE:

APRIL 1965, RON VAN CLIEF AT THE POLICE ACADEMY

My dad was an interesting man. He was one macho case. I learned how to box as a pre-teenager. One Christmas, he got me a set of boxing gloves. I learned about boxing from my brother, Larry, and my cousin Kirk. They used to beat me up all the time. I am grateful, in that, they opened the door to the martial arts for me. I don't remember much about my Dad. My father died in the Lyric Theater on Times Square. They found him when the theater closed. He died of a drug overdose. Dad was like a pirate that returned home with treasure and surprises. Pete and I would wait by the door in excitement of his return. Dad never disappointed us. He always had a surprise for us. I remember my mother and father taking me to Coney Island as a kid. My mother was afraid of the water. My father loved the ocean. Sometimes, he would take me so far out in the water I couldn't see the shore. He was a great swimmer. My Dad had a most unique talent. He was an artist. It was unbelievable the art those beaten old hands were capable of creating. Dad could draw anything. I was in southeast Asia when he died in 1964. The most horrible thing in the world is to see your father in a coffin. I will always remember watching my father drawing the female body. He had such great detail. Dad never copied anything, he drew from his mind. The symmetry and lines were almost lifelike. From him, I learned to draw. I would draw for hours and hours. I don't think my father ever knew how much I loved him.

ABOVE:

ALLAIRE VAN CLIEF, RON'S DAD

RIGHT:

DORIS VAN CLIEF AT 19 YEARS OLD, CIRCA 1940'S

Actually my mom was, and still is, a beautiful black lady. She still lives in a co-op in Brooklyn, New York. She retired from the Post Office in the 1980's, with over 15 years of dedicated service.

In Hong Kong, the Chung Wah Martial Arts Association promoted me to the level of 10th Degree Red Belt, founder of Chinese Goju. Grandmaster Leung Ting and Grandmaster Carter Wong were very influential in my early training. They introduced me to who was who in the Hong Kong martial arts scene. I studied Monkey Style kung fu with Grandmaster Chan Shou Chung, known as The Monkey King. While living in Hong Kong, I worked out at the Hong Kong Freefighting Club. During this period, I became the private student of Dr. Leung Ting. One day, I met Wang Yu in an elevator in Kowloon. He was my hero. I was in shock. Actually he was a real regular guy. Wang Yu was the top box office draw in those days, with films like *The Chinese Boxer*. Kung Fu Tak was the premiere fighter in the club. He and his brother started and ran the club. There was no kata or self defense. It was just sparring. They had a boxing ring in the middle of the room. The rest of the time, you practiced drills to music in class. You moved back and forth from left to right with the tempo of the music. Pictures of Muhammad Ali, George Foreman and Joe Frazier were displayed on the walls of the school. This was the toughest school in Kowloon for fighting. I lost several teeth and had my nose broken three times in that school. I will always remember my days at the Hong Kong Freefighting Club with fond memories. Hong Kong is wonderful place for the kung-fu student. You can find hundreds of different styles. My lifelong dream had come true. I had become a Red Belt Grand Master. The Chinese Martial Arts Association made me the Director of Kungfu to the United States. This was beyond my wildest dreams. Starring in seven films as the character The Black Dragon was unbelievable. By modern standards, I was paid almost nothing. I was paid $500 U. S. dollars per week. My food and accommodations were totally paid for. The experience was such that I would have paid them for the opportunity to star in a film. No one knew,

ABOVE:

THE MAKING OF THE
BLACK DRAGON, 1975

except Serafim Karalexis, that the Black Dragon would become an international hit. Serafim had faith in me. I traveled to Thailand, Korea, the Philippines, Taiwan and Hong Kong. The martial arts had become my way of life. I practiced everyday like a maniac. It was like an addiction. Thousands of hours in the dojo, or on the road to tournaments, gave me a type of tunnel vision. Becoming an overnight action film star was too much for me. I withdrew to the Lower East Side into a hippie like existence. In the East Village, I could practice my art without distractions. For years, I haven't had a social life. Surviving has been my social life. Staying alive!

During the late 1960's, I met Gregory Hines at the Universal Karate Championship. It was held at Robert Wagner High School. I lost the final match to Joe Hayes. Joe Hayes was Gregory's instructor. Gregory Hines was a real technician. He was a good fighter too. I remember seeing him fight at the Universal. Besides being a brilliant tap dancer, writer, actor and director he is an excellent father. If you ever see the movie, *White Nights*, you will see Gregory at his best in a choreographed martial arts and dance routine. It was one of the highlights of the movie. It is rare to see such a multi-talented individual. The study of the martial arts has definitely enhanced his life. He is a picture of physical fitness, at the young age of fifty. Gregory will get better and better as he ages. I worked on the then titled film, *White Men's Burden*. Gregory Hines was making his directorial debut. It was a learning experience, watching him work. He is a very meticulous and creative artist. The study of the martial arts could only enhance his already incredible skills. Gregory studied the Moo Duk Kwan style of Korean Karate, with Master Joe Hayes, at Richard Chun's New York school. To be a tap dancer takes incredible discipline and dedication. He was destined to be a good martial artist. Gregory is also a bodybuilder and fitness expert. For two months, I worked as the Head of Security for the movie locations. In Red Hook, Brooklyn shots were fired at the campers and trucks. We, of course, changed the location for those particular shots. After two months, we finished shooting. I am sure it will be successful with Gregory Hines at the helm. Thanks again for everything.

ABOVE:

GREGORY HINES AND RON VAN CLIEF AT CENTRAL PARK BASEBALL GAME

George Benson has been an integral part of my spiritual development. George is the consummate artist. I worked as his bodyguard on tour. He didn't know that I really loved his music. I grew up on George's music. Besides keeping George fit I taught him the art of aikijitsu, the capabilities of the soft. This art doesn't concentrate on high energy output. It stresses low energy output for high energy results. I studied the bible with George for a number of years. He taught me that God's name is Jehovah. George will always be my spiritual brother. My relationship with George was most enlightening to me. As George, Ron Jr. and myself read the Bible, we felt the peace upon us. It was unreal. The Bible was the answer to all our questions. George would come over to my Lower East Side homestead apartment when I didn't have walls. Actually George showed me how to lay sheetrock. He was smooth and quick.

He showed me how to make the seams smooth. I was a homesteader for ten years. George would come from his New Jersey home to the Lower East Side in his Mercedes. While on several tours with George, I met so many interesting people, such as Quincy Jones, Jesse Jackson, Herbie Hancock, Roberta Flack and Chaka Khan. Traveling with George was indeed a unique experience. On the road, we studied the Bible and martial arts fitness. *On Broadway* and *Masquerade* are my favorite George Benson tunes. Watching George Benson perform on stage is an enriching experience. His music makes you move. The standards that he sings reflect love and sensitivity. I have a great deal of respect for George and his music. Music is a blessing.

ABOVE:

GEORGE BENSON
AND RON VAN CLIEF

Working for Richard Pryor is a unique experience. He is funny all the time. My long time friend, Rashon Khan, was Richard's bodyguard. During the shooting of *See No Evil, Hear No Evil*, I met and started to work for Richard Pryor. Richard was truly a nice man. During my hippie drop out days in the East Village, I would occasionally see Richard at Cafe Wha or Rienzi's. He would be doing his stand up act. If you saw him in person, you would have to laugh. The man is a pure genius. Sometimes, I would see Richard and Bill Cosby in Washington Square Park. They would be doing their thing. These gentlemen are the true icons of humor in my century. In later years, I worked security for celebrities like Eddie Murphy, Magic Johnson, Ambassador Leslie Harriman of Nigeria, Quincy Jones, Jesse Jackson, Berry Gordy, Diana Ross, Jim Brown, Mike Tyson, Michael Jackson, James Brown, Wilson Pickett and Jimmy Hendricks. The East Village was very different from southeast Asia. I have never really adapted to civilian life. Almost thirty years later, I enter treatment in the Vietnam Leadership Program in New York city. It allowed me to shed some of the excess baggage I was carrying for over twenty years. When I went to the Vietnam Leadership Program, I was close to suicide. The VVLP saved my life. At the VVLP I learned that we, the black men who survived, were the real heroes.

My son Ron Jr. and I lived in an abandoned, city building for seven years. Homesteading is an enriching experience. Imagine being a single parent and building your apartment. When I say building your whole apartment, I mean it literally. I had a big hole in the floor that I temporarily covered with plywood during my eternal construction phase. Homesteading is continual maintenance. During those seven years, I learned how to sheetrock, replace pipes, windows, toilets and

ABOVE:

RICHARD PRYOR
AND RON VAN CLIEF

build several showers and bathrooms. Besides paying $50 per month rent, I was the building maintenance man. The constant harassment by government agencies was neutralized in the late 1980's. In the beginning, my son and I lived without heat and hot water. This was truly homesteading. Finally, after three years of hard work, my apartment was livable. It took seven years to have the basic systems; hot water heater, washer, dryer, gas heating unit and windows. My son, Ronnie, worked hard right beside me. He was my reason for living. From this homesteading experience, he developed the work ethic. One of my zen mission was sanding and varnishing the banisters in the six floor tenement. Several times a day, I would sweep and mop the entire building. The banisters were so polished they were slippery. Hundreds of layers of varnish and lemon oil made the banister like glass. You could actually see your reflection in the banister. During this time, I waged a one man crusade against the drug dealers. My mission was to get rid of all drug dealers in my building. I would go out in the street and take pictures of the dealers with my camera. I had a working relationship with the drug dealers, they would not deal drugs in front of my building. None of the dealers had a problem with this except the Iranian. One day he pulled a gun on me in my hallway. He pointed the gun at my face. I slapped the gun out of his hand. He ran up the stairs to his apartment. Sometimes, he would hide his drugs in the broken mail boxes. Eventually, the Iranian drug leader was arrested and

deported. Besides being shot at and stabbed, I cleaned up the street. In 1993, two bullet holes were found in my apartment door. I had been a witness against an Iranian drug dealer. He had put a contract on my life. It was no longer safe for my son and I in the East Village. This is when I decided to move to the Cayman Islands. In 1993, I moved to the Cayman Islands and worked as the Chief Instructor to the Royal Cayman Island Police Department.

LEFT:

CIRCA 1988, RON VAN CLIEF
THE HOMESTEADER

Ron Jr. grew up in the dojo. Most kids have a play room, Ronnie had the whole dojo. The weapons were his toys. At five years old, he entered the regular class. He was so energetic. Piano and violin lessons helped to develop his musical senses. It was no surprise to see he had become a great artist like his grandfather. Ronnie used to watch me draw, the same way I watched my Dad. Ronnie is twenty one and still very active in the martial arts. Taimak and Ron Jr. work out with grappling and aikijitsu techniques, on the west coast. Ron Jr., Taimak and Ralph Vicini are the foundation of the Chinese Goju System. I know Ronnie will always practice the martial arts. He has already lived the life of a real martial artist.

This headshot was the condition I was in while training for the Ultimate Fighting Championship. I recommend the Richard Simmons abdominal course for anyone interested in trimming down their midsection. I did the seven minute routine, seven days a week for nine weeks. My waist went from 34" to 31". This was great at 51 years of age. My training partner, Howard Niego, worked out with me for almost three months before the Dec. 16, 1994 UFC. I broke my ankle three weeks before the competition. My spirit made me do it anyway. I was in pain all the time. Cortisone shots and

ABOVE:

RON VAN CLIEF JR.,
THE YOUNG DRAGON
CIRCA 1981 - AIKIJITSU

RIGHT:

RETURN OF THE BLACK
DRAGON, 1994

pain pills helped me get through the Ultimate Fighting Championship. Leon Stevenson and Taimak rounded off my training in wrestling and grappling. My workout consisted of free weights and circuit training at New York's Vertical Club. It is a fantastic facility. I practiced my grappling and wrestling at Radu's Physical Culture Center, The University of the Streets, and Beach Bum Tanning Salon with Howard Niego. It was during this time that I finished writing my first draft of this book you are reading.

Mr. Michael Schultz was my mentor at the Negro Ensemble Company in the late 1960's. During this period, I worked with Douglas Turner Ward, Steve Carter, Ron O'Neal, Robert Hooks, Richard Roundtree, Arnold Johnson, Ossie Davis, Ruby Dee and a host of others. I formed the Ron Van Clief Company to tour, doing a series of martial arts vignettes. The Tiger and the Dragon combined martial arts choreography with special strobe lighting effects. My internship at the NEC allowed me to broaden my perspectives

in many areas of production. I started as a stage hand, then a lighting assistant. Eventually, I learned sound, scenery, and stage fighting. Around this time, I became a member of the East Coast Stuntmen's Association. This was it, I was hooked again. Luis Venosta wrote a screenplay, *The Last Dragon*. This film was produced by Mr. Berry Gordy. The director was Michael Schultz, my old friend and mentor. He called me one day to see if I was interested in his upcoming project. *The Last Dragon* took two years to become a reality. My student, Taimak, won the role of Bruce Leroy over thousands of potentials nationally. I told Mr. Gordy that I had just the right kid for the job. He was hesitant, because Taimak didn't have any acting experience. His gentle spirit and his incredible skills transformed Taimak into the Last Dragon. A decade or so ago, I had made the same transformation. It was wonderful to see millions of dollars spent on a black hero film. *The Last Dragon* was an international blockbuster.

ABOVE:

CIRCA 1984,
MICHAEL SCHULTZ DIRECTS
THE LAST DRAGON

It can still be seen on HBO and satellite networks around the world regularly. Michael has directed two Richard Pryor hits, *Which Way is Up* and *Car Wash*. He has such a gentle nature and quiet unassuming demeanor. *The Last Dragon* was the first major feature film starring a black hero during that decade. Michael continues to work as hard as ever. Last summer, I visited him at Warner Bros. Studio in Burbank. He was directing an episode of the sitcom *Sister, Sister*. There would have never been a Last Dragon if not for Michael's insight and creativity. Thanks for all your years of dedication. In the late 1980's, I worked on Broadway with Michael on the musical, *Mule Bone*. *Mule Bone* was my second opportunity to work on Broadway. My first was working at the Robert F. Kennedy Theater with the first Kungfu Exposition. Some of the best kungfu practi-

tioners in the world performed at the RFK Theater. I produced the "Masters in Action" special at the Orpheum Theater on 2nd Ave. It was a great show but didn't make any money. It was a great learning experience.

The 1st Japan Exposition World Championship, Grandmaster Frank Ruiz, my trainer, had worked my butt off. I was sparring everyday for about three hours. Sensei Ruiz, a former marine like myself, was a drill instructor. He said I couldn't fight my way of out of a paper bag when I met him. In seven long years, I had become the chief instructor of the black belt classes. Sometimes I would spar twenty five black belts in a row. Sensei Ruiz knocked me out twice before I fought at the Coliseum. It was a two day event. I fought eleven times. Even though this was a point tournament I was hit several times. I had to soak in a tub of ice to get ready for the second day of competition. I won first place in the Lightheavyweight division. Later on that evening, I had to fight in the round robin for the Grand Championships. This is where the different weight divisions get a chance to fight each other. After defeating the Lightweight and Heavyweight champions, I was crowned the Grand Champion. Winning first place, and Grand Champion at the World Championship, was a real mind blower. It is something I will never forget. Nothing beats the feeling of being the best, one time in your life. This was my fifteen minutes of fame. I became even more dedicated to the martial arts.

While writing my book, *The Manual of the Martial Arts,* I trained for the World Freefighting Championships in Hong Kong. I went down to 163 lbs. from 190 lbs. The tournament was quite different form what I thought it was going to be. Combatants could use any strikes they wanted. A knee in the groin or elbow strike to the face were very common techniques. The World Freefighting Championship was the prototype for shows like the Ultimate Fighting Championship. Radu and I trained at the 57th St. Dojo for nine weeks in preparation for the event. This was the first full contact, no holds barred competition I had ever fought in. I trained very hard in boxing, Kickboxing, Muay Thai and Jiujitsu. In the finals on the second day, I was knocked out by a 200 lb., Yugoslavian fighter. He kicked me in the head, while I was flat on my back on the floor. In the United States, you are not allowed to kick a downed opponent. It is totally different in the Orient. My first opponent in the elimination lasted exactly seven seconds after we engaged. I hit him with a groin kick, two monkey knees to the stomach and two left hooks to the face. He went down and I slowly walked back to my corner. I knew he couldn't continue. The referee raised my arm in victory. The crowd roared. When I was knocked out, it seemed as if I was hit by lightning. The big flashbulb went off in my brain. Short circuits were everywhere.

ABOVE:

WORLD CHAMPIONSHIPS IN HONG KONG, 1982

His instep kick hit me across the jaw and ear. The next day, my left ear looked like a prosthetic ear. It took surgery twice to restore my hearing. Initially I lost 60% of my hearing in my left ear. Acupuncture, Chinese Medicine and ear surgery returned my hearing to about 80%, which is what it is today. In over 30 years of international competition, I had many injuries, including broken teeth, broken jaw, broken nose, six broken ribs, five broken toes and five broken fingers. One time, Earl Monroe hit me and knocked two of my teeth through a hole one inch from my top lip. I could actually breathe air through the hole. Frank Ruiz broke my left leg with a round kick to the thigh. It took almost a year to return to full training. Sensei Frank Ruiz was indeed a harsh man. In 1995, I retired permanently from competition. The Ultimate Fighting Championship bout with Royce Gracie would be my finale.

This is classical Monkey Style. The Monkey grabs the fruit. Climbing and jumping techniques are integral parts of the Monkey Style. In Hong Kong, I studied elements of several monkey systems. It is a very acrobatic and physically demanding system. I studied with the Monkey King in Hong Kong in the 1970's. During this time, I met Chan Goon Tai, Fu Sheng, Wang Yu, Lo Lieh, Chang Sing, and Bolo Yeung. I remember working out at Bolo's gym in Kowloon. It was small but well equipped. Unicorn Chan was another of Bruce Lee's friends in Hong Kong. Unicorn was married to a Filipino lady. Unicorn Chan was a very nice man. He helped Bruce with the choreography for the feature, *Return of the Dragon.* I have been privileged to have trained with several Grand Masters in the Orient and the United States; Bruce Lee, Yip Man, Dr. Leung Ting, Sifu Duncan Leung, Master Leo Fong, Grandmaster Remy Presas, Grandmaster Carter Wong, Grandmaster Shimabuku, Grandmaster Latino Gonzales, Grandmaster Mat Marinas, Grandmaster Ronald Taganashi, Grandmaster Peter G. Urban, Grandmaster Moses Powell, Grandmaster Ronald Duncan, Grandmaster Steve Muhammad and Grandmaster Jimmy Jones. I owe who and what I am to these Grand Masters.

ABOVE:

THE MONKEY STYLE

Grandmaster Ron Duncan first stimulated my interests in oriental weaponry. On Okinawa, with the United States Marine Corps at Camp Sukiran in 1963, allowed me to fulfill my childhood dream of studying karate in the Orient. Grandmaster Ronald Taganashi taught me the basics of Iaido and Kendo in the 1960's. Sensei Taganashi had an extensive weapons repertoire of over 300 different traditional and contemporary forms.

Janet Bloem was one of my black belts. She trained with me five years and attained the level of black belt. At that time, I was very much in love with Janet. Janet had her film debut in *The Last Dragon*. She had a principal part and got into the Screen Actors Guild. She was excellent in gymnastics, and track and field. Janet and I lived together for three years. She moved to Puerto Rico in the 1980's.

ABOVE:

BLACK DRAGON SAMURA

LEFT:

THE BLACK DRAGON
AND THE TIGRESS, 1984

This picture was taken by Charles Bonet. We were on location filming, *The Death of Bruce Lee.* Charles Bonet and Jason Pai Piao were the good guys. They helped me to search for the reason Bruce Lee died so suddenly. Grandmaster Leung Ting really changed my martial arts life. He broadened my perspectives and philosophy. Leung Ting is the founder of the Wing Tsun Martial Arts System. He has branches all over the world numbering over one thousand. He is in constant demand for seminars and workshops. Dr. Leung Ting was the closed door student of Grandmaster Yip Man. Bruce told me to look up Sifu Leung Ting. Luckily, his school was only a few blocks from the hotel I lived in. It was wonderful. I visited every kungfu school in Kowloon at one time or another. Sifu Leung Ting and Grandmaster Carter Wong opened many doors for me in Hong Kong.

The Black Dragon's Revenge a.k.a. The Death of Bruce Lee was shot totally in Hong Kong. The shooting schedule lasted 57 days. It was really hard work. We averaged 12 to 15 hours a day at the set. Sometimes it took hours to get to the location. This was my second film in the Black Dragon series. I brought my friend and student, Master Charles Bonet, to co-star with me. It was his debut in the movie business. Charlie went on to make several kungfu action films. Jason Pai Piao was the Chinese star. He was very charismatic. I saw him in a film, *The Stranger from Canton*. This film was and is a classic. The film was directed by Yeo Ban Yee, formerly of Shaw Brothers Studios. Yeo Ban Yee and Serafim Karalexis co-produced this film. This film was a blockbuster. Yeo Ban Yee allowed me to express some of my creativity in the fight scenes. I had a great deal of respect for Yeo Ban Yee. He was an honest man. An honest man is a rarity. He will be surely missed by the world of the martial arts.

I magine being submerged in a total Chinese environment. Living with the crew in bunk beds. This film was shot completely on location in the Philippines. In the Philippines, I met President Marcos. My friend, Joseph Estrada, then Mayor of San Juan, is now the Vice-President of the Philippines. Joseph was the President of the Motion Pictures Producers of the Philippines. He was a very interesting man. His brother, George Estregan co-starred with me in this film. Being on location in the Philippines with a Chinese crew was interesting. The Chinese and the Filipino people have no love for each other. They were constantly fighting. Jason Pai Piao was the real star of this movie. I was only in the movie for 25 minutes. My character was Joe, a marine corps veteran living in the Philippines. I was a laborer on the docks. In reality, I used eight of my students to be my co-workers. One of my first black belt students, Eddie Africa a.k.a. Eddie Eng, has become a millionaire businessman. The villain was played by 22 year old Angie Hok Lin. *The Black Dragon* was a typical kungfu film of that era. Great action with simple story. I couldn't complain, my dream had come true. Imagine the Black Dragon from Brooklyn. I've been a lucky man. Luck is being in the right place at the right time. Preparation is being ready when your opportunity presents itself. Always be prepared!

ABOVE:

THE BLACK DRAGON
ON LOCATION, 1974

111

Yeo Ban Yee decided to lease me to a Korean film company to do a co-venture. I was excited to go to Korea. This was my opportunity to meet Dragon Lee. He was quite impressive. Dragon Lee introduced me to the thumb chuk. This is a single section nunchaku controlled by a ball and chain joint. On this shoot, there were many problems. One being, that I was given a car for a stunt scene that didn't have brakes. The only opportunity I had to test the breaks was as the stunt was being shot. It was a great surprise to me when I hit the brake, there was no brake pressure. The peddle went down to the floor. I proceeded with the downhill chase scene. I thought I really bought the farm this time. Imagine shooting a gun with one hand and maneuvering down a mountain road. Luckily, I got the car to stop at the bottom of the hill. I spun out of control into incoming

traffic on the highway. I escaped without injury. The driver that took the car back to the company hit a bus in route. He was hospitalized. Before I finished this film, Yeo Ban Yee had another film ready for me. I was to go to India to fight a tiger. The tiger would of course be tame. Yeo Ban Yee wanted me to fight the tiger without a shirt to show my muscles. Yeo assured me that the tiger wouldn't hurt me. After consideration, I declined the movie. Three movies in a row was hard enough. I was down to about 170 lbs., the lightest weight I had been in years. While in Korea, I got a chance to see some really good Tae Kwon Do. This movie was shot with two endings. One with Dragon Lee killing me at the end. The other with me beating Dragon Lee. The film, *Kungfu Fever* is available on video cassette all over the world.

ABOVE:

KUNG FU FEVER, 1979
SEOUL, KOREA

This shot was taken at the Wing Tsun Headquarters in Kowloon. Grandmaster Leung Ting taught most of the classes there. On this particular day, Charles Bonet and I posed for *New Martial Arts Hero* magazine. It was the first time ever that non orientals had appeared on the cover. I was very proud indeed. We had some really intensive workouts at Sifu's school. I loved to work on the wooden man. The sand bags were also one of my favorite supplementary drills. Wing Tsun is the most practical form of kungfu for street fighting. It deals with simultaneous block and counter maneuvers. Bruce Lee was a master of this form of kungfu. This particular style was created by a woman, 300 years ago in China. The style of Wing Tsun is based on the block/counter mechanism. Blocking and countering are simultaneous maneuvers. Soft blocks combined with rapid hand techniques for maximum results.

On location, filming *The Black Dragon,* in Manila. I had been to the Philippines about ten years before at Clark Air Force Base. Manila was quite wild indeed. Bars like the Texas Playhouse were infamous. George Estregan was my good friend. It was sad when he passed away in the late 1980's, a really good guy and great actor. He was highly underrated as an actor. Most of the Filipino crew spoke very little if any English. The Chinese crew spoke only Cantonese. I had a hard time trying to get things done. After a month immersed in that environment, I understood

ABOVE:

WING TSUN KWOON
GROUP SHOT, 1974,
THE WILD BUNCH

LEFT:

THE BLACK DRAGON, 1974

113

everything they said. I knew instinctively what they were saying. What a great experience. Jason Pai Piao kicked me in the head with a spinning hook kick. He almost knocked me out. I had to fake the rest of the fight scene. You really have to keep yourself centered on the set. Any mistake can result in an injury.

On location with Dragon Lee in *Kungfu Fever*. Korean films concentrated on lots of kicking techniques. It was very different from Hong Kong where they stressed hand techniques and stances. The stuntmen were very good. They were extremely stretched out and could throw kicks perpendicular to the floor, that looked great on film. The Korean stuntmen were very gymnastic. In one fight scene, I threw a stuntmen in the air with an aikijitsu technique. It was quite incredible. Actually, no one can throw someone up in the air like that. That is the wonder of filmmaking. You can create any illusion you want. In this shot, I am executing the double kick. I didn't even use the mini-trampoline. It was easy, I just jumped up and threw my legs forward, and we went to the next shot.

I broke 25 roof tiles in this break. They wanted to use fake tiles, but I insisted on using real ones. During lunch break, crew members went to get the tiles. This was a wonderful scene which allowed me to be creative. Most of the props are phony in kungfu films. Most of the weapons in this film belonged to me. In one scene, I was cut with a Butterfly Knife

on the palm of my right hand. Cinematically the scene worked very well. I have been injured on every kungfu movie I have ever worked on. Those injuries ranged from snake bites to black eyes. In the orient, there are no stunt or acting unions for kungfu action films. Actually, the companies pay the actors whatever they want. Non union films pay the actors just for the time they work. No royalties or residuals. I think I did my films for the love of the art. The martial arts was and is my life!

This shot is from the last fight scene of the film. Angie Hok Lin is the villain that I have just punched. It was great to work with some of the greatest, in my second film. After *The Black Dragon*, my co-star Jason Pai Piao said I would be the most famous black martial artist in the world. Jason, Angie and myself were a team. We moved by instinct. Both of these gentlemen were accomplished martial artists in their own systems. Angie Hok Lin and I worked very well together. He was upset because he had to shave his head. He was only twenty two years old and was playing the villain. The bald head did the job. Angie was one hell of a villain. Angie

and I worked on two films, *The Black Dragon* and *The Black Dragon's Revenge*. Jason and Angie became a matinee television idols in Hong Kong. In the film, *Stranger from Canton*, Jason was the good guy and Thompson Kao Kong was the villain. Thompson Kao Kong was the supervillain in *The Black Dragon's Revenge*. Jason and Thomspon played medieval rivals dueling for the finale. Thompson had the long, Mandarin tail and used it as a weapon. The sound effects made the hair sound like a whip. He even killed several ninja with his hair. That film was, and is, my all time favorite of the 1970's kungfu films. This is the film that made me want to become a kungfu movie star. Sometimes wishes can come true! You just have to work very hard also. The process is

ABOVE:

CIRCA 1974,
THE DEATH OF BRUCE LEE

to get the best you can at what you do. Hard work combined with being in the right place at the right time. Remember you have to be prepared for the job. Going to Hong Kong to make movies was one of the biggest challenge of my life.

The Black Dragon and Dragon Lee on location in Korea. Dragon Lee was a really good actor. He could have been a comedian. His skills as a martial artist were incredible. We would share ideas and principles about fighting techniques. His background was in Hapkido and Tae Kwon Do. I learned the thumb chuk from Dragon Lee when we filmed, *Kungfu Fever.* Pusan was a beautiful city by the sea. I went to a local tournament and saw some very intricate aerial breaking maneuvers. It was quite an inspiring trip, to say the least. This was the first time that I worked with a non-Chinese team. Each country that I worked in had a different operating procedure for film making. The actors and stunt personnel have to change according to the directors they work for. American film producers are putting martial arts in all the action films these days. Martial arts has replaced the old John Wayne type of punching. I have always been an action film junkie. Today martial arts can be employed with a myriad of special computer generated effects. The overall

presentation of martial arts can be brought to a higher level. No matter what the special effect, it is the actor or stunt person that makes the action look realistic. In Hong Kong, I learned how to choreograph martial arts for film. There were many problems on the set. Language problems were the biggest of the problems. The action director was very receptive to my ideas regarding choreography. I did more kicking in this film than any of the films in my whole career. They literally worked my butt off. On location, I drank some water from a water fountain. It made me so sick, I was hospitalized. From that point on, I only drank bottled water. This was my first and only film shooting on location in Korea. Maybe someday I will get the opportunity to go back to Korea on vacation.

On location for *The Death of Bruce Lee,* in Hong Kong. In this scene, the police come to the Black Dragon temple to tell me that Charlie "The Panther" is dead. This is the revenge part of the movie. I am honor bound to find the killer of Charlie. Charlie is played by Master Charles Bonet. During the early 1960's, I first met Charlie on the island of Okinawa.

We served our country in the United States Marine Corps. Charles Bonet is the founder of Kun Tao, an eclectic form of martial arts. Charlie went on to make several more movies. This was my second starring role as the Black Dragon. Charlie and I went directly to Thailand to make *The Way of the Black Dragon.* We had a really good fight scene at the end of *The Way of the Black Dragon.* It's too bad I had to kill him in the movie. Charlie was the first Latino kungfu movie star. Later that year, we did the documentary, *The Super Weapon.* I haven't seen Charlie since we worked on *The Super Weapon* together. We both got our dragon and panther tattoos at Jimmy Woo's Tattoo Parlor. My dragon tattoo took almost two hours to put on. Charlie's took forty-five minutes. The next day, while practicing the fight scenes, we were both bloody. My left forearm is sensitive even today. I missed getting my tattoo in Saigon and got it in Hong Kong. The symbol of the dragon was my sign. Charlie was the panther. The tattoo has a very different meaning to the martial artist.

ABOVE:

CIRCA 1975,
THE DEATH OF BRUCE LEE

On location in the Philippines shooting the action film, *The Bamboo Trap*. My mentor and friend, Leo Fong was the star of the film. He wanted me to do a cameo in his film. I was supposed to work for one week. Due to problems with weather and crew, I remained on the shoot for one month. Even though I only made one thousand dollars, I was happy to do it for Leo Fong. Leo Fong is a master of Hung Gar and Choy Lai Fut. I learned realistic kickboxing from Leo. One day, he gave me a black eye while sparring in our hotel. Darnell Garcia was the co-star and villain. Our final fight scene lasted at least ten minutes. It took two days to film. In the final scene of this movie, I was tied to a cross. They put bamboo splints under my fingernails. Laying on that cross was the hardest thing. After thirty minutes on the cross, I wanted to go to the hotel and take a hot bath. Leo came to save the day. Leo and I kill all the bad guys at the end of the movie. Leo Fong is an incredible martial artist and my good friend. I learned a great deal from Leo about full contact fighting. He believed in weight training to improve martial skills. Leo was absolutely right. Previous to this, I believed that weights made you stiff. Leo Fong had been a boxer earlier in his career. That explains the great right hook. When I finished this movie, I stayed in the Philippines with Grandmaster Remy Presas. Grandmaster Presas is the founder of Modern Arnis. Modern Arnis is the traditional style of blade, stick and hand defense in the Philippines. From Remy, I learned the basics principles of Modern Arnis. I attained the rank of Lakan Pito in Modern Arnis certified by Grandmaster Presas. When you meet a great master like Remy Presas, they introduce you to the very best. The martial arts is alive and well in the Philippines. On Sunday mornings, I would go to Luneta Park to spar and learn some techniques. There would be thousands of people doing martial arts. You could see all of the different styles of martial arts practiced. It was really a great experience for me. I thank God for all of my blessings.

ABOVE:

CIRCA 1976,
THE BAMBOO TRAP

118

This is another shot from *The Bamboo Trap.* I am actually on the cross. In my hand, I have a long piece of bamboo that I use as a weapon. I throw one through the neck of a villain. One day, Joseph Estrada came to the set. He was the President of

the Motion Picture Producers Association. Now he is the Vice-President of the Philippines. He was a great actor and I believe he will be a great Vice-President. Darnell Garcia who is a Chuck Norris protégé was a great villain. He really looked the part. Darnell had a small part in Bruce Lee's *Enter the Dragon.* Darnell and I had some very unique sparring sessions. One day, Leo had to break us up. It seemed we both got carried away. The director, Mr. Eddie Garcia was a real big director in the Philippines. He was quite a creative and innovative director.

In September of 1977, I traveled to West Africa. My student, Sensei Danny Gwira taught Chinese Goju in Ghana. This was my first opportunity to see Africa. My mission was to travel around West Africa and spread the doctrine of the Black Dragon. Within a year, I had nine hundred students just in Accra. We hired a bus

ABOVE:

CIRCA 1976,
THE BAMBOO TRAP

LEFT:

CIRCA 1977,
THE BLACK DRAGON
IN GHANA

119

and traveled from Accra to Sekondi Takoradi, Kumasi, Togo and the Ivory Coast. Most of our demonstrations were at movie theaters. At the end of the show, I would accept challenges from the audience. Sometimes the fighters would become over zealous. At one theater, I kicked a challenger with a side kick right into the audience. The audience went wild. West Africa is beautiful. It was really like coming home. I was treated like someone. Not just a movie star, but a brother. I will never forget my experiences in Ghana, especially in 1979, when they had the coup. Now President, Jerry Rawlings, was in jail. The revolutionaries took him out of jail. I had the honor of meeting him before I left Accra. Africa will always be at the foundation of my roots.

This photograph was taken at Radu's Physical Culture Center in New York City. We had one of the 1000 kick classes. George Benson and I were practicing some aikijitsu. Due to a knee injury, I was taking it easy. Taimak was leading the class. The day before, I had micro surgery on my left knee. Knee injuries take a long time to heal. My left knee has never worked right since that surgery. The therapy is the hardest part of the recovery. You have to be able to overcome pain. Pain is the best teacher. That is what Grandmaster Peter Urban taught me to believe. The majority of my injuries were because of sparring. Sparring is not mandatory. It is only one area of martial arts education. Today, you have to wear protective equipment when you spar. Remember that sparring has nothing to do with real self defense. Martial arts can be a great exercise for the mind and body. You can practice the martial arts, and never have to spar. All sparring must be done under supervision. People never attack you the way you are attacked in sparring. There are no rules in the street. Many actors and actresses train with me at Radu's, because the students know that I will not injure them. A student should never be injured in training. Most want to learn simple movements that will be useful on the street. Aerobic Self Defense is what I teach today. We practice aerobic martial arts movements to music. This becomes a good cardiovascular exercise. When you practice to music, you don't think about fatigue. You practice proper breathing with techniques. To me, martial arts is the best exercise in the world, bar none.

ABOVE:

CIRCA 1982, GEORGE BENSON, TAIMAK AND RON VAN CLIEF

In conclusion, I wrote this book out of respect for the black heroes of the martial arts. These men and women have dedicated their lives to the arts. We do this not for money, but for the sheer love of the arts. This book would not have been completed if not for the dedication of Dorria Ameen. She has made this book a reality. Thank you, Dorrie! There are not enough pages in this book to include all the black heroes. With luck, I will be able to do another volume. In such a hostile environment, we are all heroes. Lastly, I would like to thank all my friends and adversaries for giving me the motivation to write this oral history of blacks in the martial arts. Knowledge is not yours until you give it to somebody! May the history and legend of the black heroes live forever!

ABOVE:

THE OFFICIAL RON VAN CLIEF CHINESE GOJU PATCH

LEFT:

CIRCA 1974, THE BLACK DRAGON'S REVENGE

OVERLEAF:

RON VAN CLIEF, FOUNDER, THE CHINESE GOJU SYSTEM

INDEX

124